WORLD HISTORY

PIRACY

FROM THE HIGH SEAS
TO THE DIGITAL AGE

By Jennifer Lombardo

Portions of this book originally appeared in *Piracy on the High Seas* by Diane Yancey.

LUCENT
P R E S S

Published in 2019 by
Lucent Press, an Imprint of Greenhaven Publishing, LLC
353 3rd Avenue
Suite 255
New York, NY 10010

Designer: Deanna Paternostro
Editor: Jennifer Lombardo

Cataloging-in-Publication Data

Names: Lombardo, Jennifer.
Title: Piracy: from the high seas to the digital age / Jennifer Lombardo.
Description: New York : Lucent Press, 2019. | Series: World history | Includes index.
Identifiers: ISBN 9781534563841 (pbk.) | ISBN 9781534563827 (library bound) | ISBN 9781534563834 (ebook)
Subjects: LCSH: Pirates—Juvenile literature. | Piracy—Juvenile literature.
Classification: LCC G535.L66 2019 | DDC 364.16'4—dc23

Printed in the United States of America

CPSIA compliance information: Batch #BS18KL: For further information contact Greenhaven Publishing LLC, New York, New York at 1-844-317-7404.

Please visit our website, www.greenhavenpublishing.com. For a free color catalog of all our high-quality books, call toll free 1-844-317-7404 or fax 1-844-317-7405.

Contents

Foreword

History books are often filled with names and dates—words and numbers for students to memorize for a test and forget once they move on to another class. However, what history books should be filled with are great stories, because the history of our world is filled with great stories. Love, death, violence, heroism, and betrayal are not just themes found in novels and movie scripts. They are often the driving forces behind major historical events.

When told in a compelling way, fact is often far more interesting—and sometimes far more unbelievable—than fiction. World history is filled with more drama than the best television shows, and all of it really happened. As readers discover the incredible truth behind the triumphs and tragedies that have impacted the world since ancient times, they also come to understand that everything is connected. Historical events do not exist in a vacuum. The stories that shaped world history continue to shape the present and will undoubtedly shape the future.

The titles in this series aim to provide readers with a comprehensive understanding of pivotal events in world history. They are written with a focus on providing readers with multiple perspectives to help them develop an appreciation for the complexity of the study of history. There is no set lens through which history must be viewed, and these titles encourage readers to analyze different viewpoints to understand why a historical figure acted the way they did or why a contemporary scholar wrote what they did about a historical event. In this way, readers are able to sharpen their critical-thinking skills and apply those skills in their history classes. Readers are aided in this pursuit by formally documented quotations and annotated bibliographies, which encourage further research and debate.

Many of these quotations come from carefully selected primary sources, including diaries, public records, and contemporary research and writings. These valuable primary sources help readers hear the voices of those who directly experienced historical events, as well as the voices of biographers and historians who provide a unique perspective on familiar topics. Their voices all help history come alive in a vibrant way.

As students read the titles in this series, they are provided with clear context in the form of maps, timelines, and informative text. These elements give them the basic facts they need to fully appreciate the high drama that is history.

The study of history is difficult at times—not because of all the information that needs to be memorized, but because of the challenging questions it asks us. How could something as horrible as the Holocaust happen? Why would religious leaders use torture during the Inquisition? Why does ISIS have so many followers? The information presented in each title gives readers the tools they need to confront these questions and participate in the debates they inspire.

As we pore over the stories of events and eras that changed the world, we come to understand a simple truth: No one can escape being a part of history. We are not bystanders; we are active participants in the stories that are being created now and will be written about in history books decades and even centuries from now. The titles in this series help readers gain a deeper appreciation for history and a stronger understanding of the connection between the stories of the past and the stories they are part of right now.

SETTING THE SCENE: A TIMELINE

| 2000–1100 BC | 1518 | 1650–1730 | 1801–1805 |

Aruj Barbarossa dies, and his brother, Hizir, inherits his position as governor general of the western Mediterranean, making him one of the most powerful privateers in history.

The Golden Age of Piracy, in which pirates were most active and acquired the most treasure, takes place.

The First Barbary War is fought between the United States and Tripoli.

The Vedas, sacred texts that mention piracy in India, are written.

More than 20 countries join forces to create the Combined Task Force 151, an organization that fights piracy.

Zheng Yi Sao takes over her husband's pirate empire and becomes one of the most successful female pirates in history.

Federal judges rule that having the IP address of a computer that downloaded content illegally is not enough proof to charge the owner of that computer with digital piracy.

onfig

s IP Configuration

rnet adapter server:

Connection-specific DNS Suffix . . . . :
IP Address. . . . . :
Subnet Mask . . . . :
Default Gateway . . . . :

MYTHS VERSUS REALITY

For years, pirates have been figures of adventure and excitement. Movies such as the Pirates of the Caribbean franchise have become incredibly popular, pirate costumes are a common sight at Halloween, and September 19 has been designated the official Talk Like a Pirate Day. However, many people are unaware of the realities of pirate life throughout the ages. Even fewer know that pirates are still active today, mainly along the coasts of Asia and Africa.

Since the rise of the internet, the word "piracy" has also come to mean the practice of illegally making songs, movies, and other media available online for free. Many people do not see a problem with this, but the fact is that internet piracy hurts a country's economy and carries harsh penalties, such as high fines or jail time, for people who are caught illegally uploading or downloading media.

Historical Piracy

There has been piracy on the high seas since ships first began to sail the oceans. The Vedas, ancient Indian texts dating from 2000 to 1100 BC, speak of pirate attacks that took place early in that country's history. In the 12th and 13th centuries BC, seafaring raiders known as the Sea Peoples plundered Egyptian ships in the Middle East.

No matter when or where it occurs, maritime piracy is defined as robbery or criminal acts of violence committed on any major body of water and the land edging that water. It can involve taking cargo, hijacking an entire ship, or holding passengers for ransom, and it always happens for reasons of personal profit. This is what makes piracy different from maritime terrorism, which is committed for political reasons. The bombing of the USS *Cole* on October 12, 2000, for instance, was an example of

Today, pirates are often shown as harmless or funny, but in the past, they were feared.

maritime terrorism. In that incident, nothing was stolen, but 17 sailors were killed. The terrorist group al-Qaeda claimed responsibility for the attack.

Despite the fact that piracy generally involves violence and theft, it is often seen as being part of an adventurous, fascinating, and idealized way of life. Early pirates were feared, but they were also often secretly admired. They were considered brave and strong. They dared to ignore the laws of polite society. Most important, pirates enjoyed total freedom. They traveled around the world in control of their own lives. In the words of historian Peter Earle, they "sailed their beautiful ships through beautiful tropical seas before running down a prize [ship] and swinging aboard with astonishing agility and ferocity."[1]

Romanticizing Piracy

In the 19th and 20th centuries, novels and Hollywood movies often emphasized the glamour of piracy. In books such as Robert Louis Stevenson's *Treasure Island*, pirates buried chests of treasure and carried parrots on their shoulders. Older Hollywood movies showed the outlaws as handsome, well mannered, and generous, especially to

Ancient Indian texts, such as the one shown here, mention pirate raids on India from 2000 BC.

women and the poor. Author James Robert Parish described a fictional movie pirate as "a man fighting for the right in a world that does not understand the right as he sees it."[2]

However, fictional stories often leave out certain details, especially when the pirates are supposed to be the "good guys." In real life, pirates broke laws and often killed people while carrying out attacks. Unlike their fictional counterparts, many pirates were mean and cruel to outsiders, although they could be kind to their crewmates and sometimes their prisoners. Author Edward E. Leslie wrote of one pirate, Edward Low,

"The psychopath's history … is filled with mutilations, disembowelings, decapitations, and slaughter."[3]

Fictional pirates were also portrayed as independent adventurers, but piracy was frequently big business. A ruler or corrupt government official who wanted to make money or undermine a rival country's economy often made it financially worthwhile for men to go into piracy. Queen Elizabeth I supported Francis Drake in attacking and stealing from Spanish ships in the 1570s; royal governor of Pennsylvania William Markham and royal governor of New York Benjamin Fletcher encouraged

ROBERT LOUIS STEVENSON'S
TREASURE ISLAND

:: ARTHUR BOURCHIER ::
As "LONG JOHN SILVER."

Pirates are a common and beloved part of popular culture.

treasure, or wear fancy clothes. Additionally, ships that were targeted by historical pirates tended to belong to rich merchants or to a government. While a pirate attack was not pleasant for the crews that manned these ships, they were often prepared to fight and could afford to lose some of their cargo if they could not defend it. While modern pirates have some of the same targets, they also tend to attack individuals; it is the maritime equivalent of robbing someone's house. They also sometimes kidnap these individuals and hold them for ransom.

Internet pirates are another thing entirely. They do not operate on the ocean; anyone with an internet connection can illegally download media or make it available for others to download. According to study results reported in *Tech Times*, about 57 million Americans report acquiring music illegally. Although some said they did it because they did not want to pay for their music, others said they purchased some songs and downloaded others. About 80 percent of survey respondents said they did

and financially backed pirates in America in the 1690s. Backing pirates was technically illegal for rulers, but it was less expensive and less politically risky than waging a true war.

Current maritime pirates, however, are generally not seen as glamorous figures. They do not sail large ships, bury

this when they liked a song but not enough to pay for it.

However, the ideals of freedom and fighting for justice that were applied to historical pirates are sometimes also applied to internet pirates. Some people believe media should not be as expensive as it is and see making it available for free as a way to hurt large corporations, which they tend to believe take advantage of both their customers and their employees. These people may not always realize that their actions may be driving prices up and negatively affecting artists, actors, and other individuals.

What a Pirate Needs

For piracy to take place throughout history, many elements had to be present. First, the pirates needed to be able to count on maritime trade routes through which merchant ships regularly passed. There had to be places on those routes where no nearby law enforcement ships could interfere with a pirate's attack.

Pirates also needed hideouts—bays, coves, and rivers—and trading posts where they could resupply their ships and dispose of stolen goods. Internet pirates, of course, do not need a physical hideout, but they do need ways to make their online activities untraceable to law enforcement.

The ideal maritime piracy conditions existed in the Mediterranean and the Caribbean in early times, and they exist in West Africa and Southeast Asia today. Piracy was a problem in the past, and it is a growing problem in the modern world. Although maritime pirates have given up sailing ships for modern motorboats and cutlasses for automatic weapons, they remain ruthless and lawless, ready to steal and take lives. "Piracy is not a thing of the past, a romanticized form of crime from the pages of history," said pirate expert Angus Konstam. "It still happens every day, and the victims don't always live to tell the tale."[4]

CHAPTER ONE

PIRACY IN THE MEDITERRANEAN

Piracy has been a problem on the North African coast for centuries. In the past, the Barbary pirates were the main danger; this was the name for any pirate who operated in North Africa. According to *Encyclopedia Britannica*, Barbary pirates were "at their most powerful during the 17th century but still active until the 19th century."[5] Some of these pirates were outlaws who operated individually, attacked ships of any country, and kept stolen goods for themselves. Over time, these types of pirates were called sea thieves, sea rovers, freebooters, and swashbucklers. Former librarian Cindy Vallar explained where some of these names came from:

> In the 1800s, authors translated the Dutch word vrijbuiter *into freebooter, a person who searched for ill-gotten gains … When [the word]* swashbuckler *first appeared in writings of the 16th century, it referred to someone who made a loud noise by striking his sword against his shield. Today the word often refers to pirates or movies about them.*[6]

A second group of pirates was known as privateers. They were loyal to their country of choice and stole for their sponsor, who could be a wealthy merchant or a king or queen. They carried official letters of marque, which entitled them to attack and loot the ships of enemy countries. Their efforts enhanced weak royal navies and helped fill royal treasuries. They gave their loot to the sponsor and received a generous portion as a reward for their services. Privateers had a semi-legal status in the world, and their countrymen saw them as heroes. To their enemies, of course, they were viewed as outlaws.

Danger on the Mediterranean Sea

Both types of pirates looted in the Mediterranean Sea over the centuries. Details

IGNORING THE FACTS

Novelists and film producers mix fact and fiction when creating their books and movies. In his book *Under the Black Flag*, author David Cordingly pointed out:

> *More than seventy films have been made about pirates, buccaneers and corsairs. While some film directors and producers have gone to considerable lengths to build pirate ships, stage elaborate sea battles, and film in appropriate locations … it is curious how few of the films follow the historical events with any accuracy. Most are based on works of fiction, or plunder the histories of the real pirates with a … disregard for the facts. There is nothing wrong with this … But the fact remains that the lives of some of the real pirates and the men who hunted them down are as fascinating and as full of drama as any of the works of fiction.[1]*

1. David Cordingly, *Under the Black Flag: The Romance and the Reality of Life Among the Pirates.* New York, NY: Random House, 1995, p. 177.

are incomplete and confusing in some areas because it was so long ago. For example, many names have multiple spellings, and some pirates used the same name, making it difficult in some cases to tell who did what. However, many basic details are known.

The Thracians and Illyrians, who lived in what is now Albania and Montenegro in the Western Balkans, were so dangerous in 230 BC that the Roman Empire went to war to wipe them out. Turkish privateers from the Ottoman Empire also plagued the region from the 16th to the 19th centuries.

There were many reasons why the Mediterranean was a hot spot of piracy. Mountains prevented easy overland passage between Asia and Europe, so the main lines of communication and trade were by sea. Merchant ships that traveled on the Mediterranean generally followed established routes that were close to the coast. That made it relatively easy for sea thieves to plan and carry out attacks. While ships filled with valuable cargo sailed on the Mediterranean, people living on its coastline were poor. Their land was barren and rocky. It could not support large-scale farming, so any villages that developed were small. Inhabitants relied on fishing for income, but when fishing was bad, they had to look for other ways to make a living. Most able-bodied men had boats

Pirates who had bases on the coast of North Africa were called Barbary pirates, but they were not the only kind of pirates to sail the Mediterranean Sea. This map shows the region around this body of water in ancient times.

and were at home on the sea, and so, for some, piracy became a source of income that gave them more wealth than fishing alone.

Piracy and Religion

Piracy in the Mediterranean was not just motivated by money, it was also motivated by religious differences. The Roman Empire—the most powerful political force in Europe between 27 BC and AD 395—adopted Christianity as its official religion in AD 380. During the early Middle Ages (AD 500 to 1000), most of the people of Europe and the area around the Mediterranean were Christians.

However, the Roman Empire did not last forever. As its power began waning, Turkish influence grew in the Mediterranean. The Turks originated in Asia and migrated westward beginning in the 11th century, bringing the Islamic religion with them. The powerful Ottoman Empire was established in 1265, and by the 16th and 17th centuries, it encompassed much of southeastern Europe, western Asia, and northern Africa. The Ottomans were Muslim, and because of differing religious beliefs and a desire to expand their empire, they were often in conflict with Christian empires.

Muslim privateers, also known as corsairs, helped carry out Ottoman

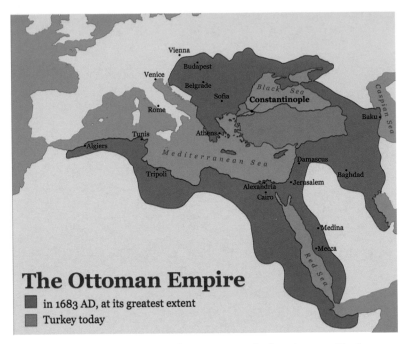

The Ottoman Empire

■ in 1683 AD, at its greatest extent
■ Turkey today

The Ottoman Empire, which grew out of what is now Turkey, had a lot of influence on ancient Europe.

dreams of conquest. They captured merchant ships from countries such as Spain, stealing the treasure and holding the ships and crews for ransom. Since they were acting under the orders of the leader of the Ottoman Empire, their actions were seen as lawful.

A Belief in Righteousness

Corsair activity was sponsored by local government leaders in North Africa. North Africa was also known as the Barbary Coast, after the Berber tribespeople who originally lived there. During the reign of the Ottoman Empire, it was divided into states called the Regency of Algiers, Tunis, Tripolitania, and the kingdom of Morocco (present-day Algeria, Tunisia, Libya, and Morocco). Rulers of these states gave their allegiance to the Ottoman leader, or sultan, but were essentially independent. Sometimes they were even former pirates who had captured a region and continued to send their associates out to plunder enemy shipping.

Local merchants and wealthy businessmen also often supported corsair activity because they believed that it was a good way to make a profit and please God at the same time by helping support the spread of Islam. They gave the pirates ships and supplies, and at the end of a raid, they received a share of the treasure that had been taken. An additional 10 percent of any profits went to the supporting government.

Muslim corsairs were not the only ones who fought for their faith in the Mediterranean. Maltese corsairs were Catholic privateers authorized by the Knights of St. John, a Christian military order who lived on the island of Malta in the middle of the Mediterranean. Although small in number, the Maltese corsairs were fearless men who had

The Maltese cross, shown here, was a symbol used by the Knights of St. John.

the reputation of attacking and overcoming huge fleets of Muslim ships. In the words of historian Peter Earle, they were "driven by a desire for profit ... but also driven by religious zeal and a lust for adventure and glory."[7] Although the pirates of Barbary and Malta were enemies, they were, in fact, similar to one another. They were business-like, organized, motivated, and very determined to defeat the enemies of their faiths.

A Pirate's Transportation

While Christian corsairs called Malta their home, the Barbary corsairs had their bases in the port of Algiers and the Moroccan port of Salé. Both were walled cities with natural harbors that provided shelter for ships. Both served as excellent home bases from which to launch attacks. Setting out from these harbors, the corsairs preyed on vessels in the western Mediterranean as well as on ships sailing around Africa on their way to Asia.

The corsairs often traveled in convoys, or groups, of ships, and their ships of choice were galleys—light, narrow vessels that could be easily maneuvered in shallow water. Galleys sometimes had triangular sails, but they were propelled by dozens of men—generally slaves—who sat on benches in tiers and pulled long oars all together. In the words of former galley slave Jean Marteille de Bergerac, "Think of six men chained to a bench, naked as when they were born ... holding an immensely heavy oar, bending forwards to the stern with arms at full reach to clear the backs of the rowers in front."[8] Later, square-masted sailing ships, which were common in Europe, were introduced to the Mediterranean pirates. Square-masted ships were generally faster and more stable than galleys and allowed the pirates to travel greater distances into the ocean. Authors Stanley Lane-Poole and James Douglas Jerrold Kelley noted another benefit: "A long cruise is impossible in a galley, where you have some hundreds of rowers to feed, and where each pound of biscuit adds to the labor of motion; but sails have no mouths and can carry along a great weight of provisions without getting tired ... So sails triumphed over oars."[9]

The rest of the crew was often made up of a collection of renegade men from countries all around the Mediterranean.

For many years, galleys similar to this one were the ship of choice for Barbary pirates.

These included Janissaries—soldiers from the Ottoman military who had been recruited by promises of riches. They did not do work on the ship; they simply waited until another ship was captured, then boarded it to take their loot.

Pirate Attack!

While on the hunt for victims, corsairs disguised their galleys as merchant ships. They covered their guns, and instead of flying the flag of their home country, which was often closely associated with piracy, they flew a false flag as they approached their victim. Then, when they were close enough, they fired off their cannons and, if necessary, smashed into the other ship with a battering ram mounted on the bow, or front, of their vessel. Immediately after, a large boarding party swept onto the merchant ship, screaming and shouting curses, and waving muskets, swords, pikes (sharp blades attached to long sticks), and knives. The surprise and terror of the attack was generally enough to cause the merchant ship to surrender quickly. If not, the pirates attacked with their weapons until the crew was overpowered.

THE BUSINESS OF SLAVERY

Barbary pirates did not just take valuable items from ships. They also often captured people to keep or sell as slaves. Individuals captured by Barbary corsairs were made slaves for life unless someone purchased their freedom. As Angus Konstam wrote in *Piracy: The Complete History*,

> The only hope for many of the poorer captives was that some Christian religious order would buy their freedom. One of these groups—the Redemptionists—organized the purchase and freedom of some 15,500 Christian slaves of all nationalities between 1575 and 1769. Another Catholic organization called the Lazarists were equally successful. Sometimes governments took a hand in the business of raising money. For example, in 1643, seven women petitioned the English Parliament to allow churches to take up collections because "Their husbands and others were taken by Turkish pirates, carried to Algiers, and there now remain in miserable captivity, having great fines imposed on them for their ransoms."[1]

1. Angus Konstam, *Piracy: The Complete History*. New York, NY: Osprey, 2008, p. 92.

Once a ship was captured, it was taken back to land, where the cargo was unloaded and the crew held for ransom or sold as slaves. The use of slave labor was common in the Ottoman Empire, and it is estimated that between 1 million and 1.25 million non-Muslim people around the Mediterranean were enslaved by corsairs between 1530 and 1780. The only way captured crew members could hope to escape such treatment was if someone paid a ransom for them or if they converted to Islam.

Pirates also found victims for the slave markets from villages along the Mediterranean coastline. This caused enormous fear because no one could tell when there would be a raid on their area, with men, women, and children being kidnapped. The corsairs were so feared that many coastal inhabitants moved inland, leaving long stretches of coast in Spain and Italy almost completely abandoned.

The Barbarossa Brothers

There were hundreds of Barbary corsairs, but none were as famous as the Barbarossa brothers, who were known for their red hair and beards. The brothers' names are often seen spelled several different ways, depending on which source and language they are found in: Aruj, Arouj, Uruj, or Oruc for the older one, and Khizr, Khidr, or Hizir for the younger one. They became known as the Barbarossa brothers after becoming infamous in Europe. Aruj was sometimes called Baba Aruj, which Italians thought sounded similar to *barba rossa*, literally "red beard" in Italian. Since he did have a red beard, the name stuck to both brothers. They were born in Greece in the 1460s or 1470s and were sailors before they became pirates. Once they took to pirating, they were so clever and daring that they became the most successful corsairs of the Barbary Coast, with hundreds of men joining their pirate convoy. They had two other brothers, one of whom worked with them until he was killed in a battle with a rival ship and the other of whom stayed at home to work in the family business.

The brothers were given 18 galleys by the Ottoman ruler and told to fight the Knights of St. John, who were doing much damage to Ottoman merchant ships. This was only the start of their adventures. Between 1503 and 1516, they fought against rival ships from many nations and established bases in the Mediterranean as well as their own fleet of captured ships. In 1516, while fighting off a Spanish attack on Algiers, Aruj took the opportunity to seize the city from its ruler and declare himself sultan of Algiers. He then gave up his title and swore loyalty to the Ottomans in return for their help in beating back the Spanish. For his act of loyalty, he was appointed governor general of the western Mediterranean by Ottoman sultan Selim I. Konstam noted that this made him "de facto [unofficial] ruler of the Barbary coast."[10]

Despite his skill and experience, Aruj was killed while fighting a fleet of galleys sent by Holy Roman Emperor Charles V in

HORU5CE und HAREADEN BARBAROSSA
Könige von Tunis und Algiers, und ober See Admiralen.

The Barbarossa brothers are two of the most famous Barbary pirates.

1518. During his career as a pirate, the older Barbarossa brother had proved to be a sizable threat to the Holy Roman Empire. Authors Lane-Poole and Kelley wrote, "He resided in Barbary fourteen years, during which time the harms he did to the Christians are inexpressible."[11]

Keeping It in the Family

After Aruj's death, Hizir Barbarossa, also known as Kheyr-ed-din or Hayreddin—a title said to have been given to him by Selim I's son, Sultan Suleiman the Magnificent—took over his older brother's position as governor general and continued attacking ships, plundering coastlines, and capturing slaves off the southern coast of France, the Balearic Islands, and Spain.

Hayreddin became known as master of the Mediterranean and the enemy of Christian sailors. He was eventually given command of the entire Ottoman navy and won many battles, including a fight against a Christian fleet in 1538 where the Christians outnumbered the Turks by at least three to one. The defeat secured the eastern Mediterranean for the Ottomans for the next 30 years. As a result of this victory, Hayreddin was a prominent figure of the sultan's court in Constantinople. He remained there until his death in 1546 and was buried in Istanbul (formerly Constantinople), Turkey, where his statue stands today near the Turkish Naval Museum.

Joining the Turks

Corsairs who came from Greece, Turkey, and Albania were not the only pirates who looted the Mediterranean. English pirates and privateers such as Richard Bishop and Henry Mainwaring also entered the ranks of the Barbary pirates beginning in the early 1600s. They were motivated by greed and sometimes by the need to escape their home countries because they had broken the law.

Those Europeans who gave up their original roots and loyalties to adopt a life of piracy in the Mediterranean were said to have "turned Turk." Some of them even converted to Islam and took Middle Eastern names. For example, Dutch-born sailor Jan Janszoon van Haarlem was captured by Barbary corsairs and taken to Algiers as a captive in 1618. Changing his loyalty to the corsairs, Janszoon became known as Murat Reis and sailed for a time with other Dutch-born Barbary pirates. He then led a dreaded band of pirates known as the Salee Rovers, who operated from the stronghold of Salé. While sailing off the coast of Tunis in 1635, Janszoon was captured by members of the Knights of Malta and spent five years in a dungeon, where he was mistreated and tortured. He escaped in 1640 and returned to Morocco, where he retired from piracy.

An English Convert

One of the most notorious European pirates in the Mediterranean was an Englishman known as Captain Jack

CAPTAIN JACK SPARROW

Captain Jack Sparrow, the famous and beloved character from the Pirates of the Caribbean movies, has been rumored to have been based on Captain Jack Birdy. The connection between the names is easy to see, and some have noted similarities in the ways the two Jacks acted and dressed. However, this has not been confirmed either by the creators of the character or Johnny Depp, the actor who played him. According to Depp, his inspiration came from a combination of musician Keith Richards and Pepe LePew, a cartoon skunk from the television show *Looney Tunes*.

Some people have suggested that the character of Captain Jack Sparrow is based on Captain Jack Birdy, but this has not been confirmed by Disney or Johnny Depp.

Birdy, who was born John Ward and later became known as Yusuf Reis. In the words of Sir Henry Wotton, the English ambassador to Venice, Italy, in 1607, "Ward, so well-known in this port for the damage he has done, is beyond a doubt the greatest scoundrel that ever sailed from England."[12]

Little is known of Ward's early life, but some accounts say he started out as a fisherman and later became a privateer in the service of the British government. When King James I took the throne in 1603 and ended privateering, Ward was forced to join the Royal Navy to make ends meet. However, he hated the discipline and the low pay of the navy, so he soon convinced some of his shipmates to desert and help him steal a boat. They sailed to Tunis, where they turned to piracy. Ward was both talented and lucky; each ship he captured proved more valuable than the last. He ended up a wealthy man but was unable to return to England because of his lawlessness, so he converted to Islam and settled in Tunis. There he built a palace with his riches. He died of the plague in 1622.

In addition to his notorious reputation, Ward gained fame for introducing the corsairs to square-masted sailing ships, which were common in Europe. Square-masted ships were generally faster and more stable than galleys and allowed the pirates to travel greater distances into the ocean.

Paying for Protection

With the latest in European sailing innovation and the powerful backing of the Ottoman Empire, the Barbary corsairs were virtually uncontrollable. European powers such as Britain, France, Spain, and the Netherlands might have cooperated to end their control, but these countries were political and commercial rivals. If Spanish ships were attacked,

the British were happy, and vice versa. With no good solution to the problem, a compromise was finally reached. Countries such as Britain agreed to pay an annual sum of money to each Barbary Coast ruler. In return, that ruler's corsairs would not attack that country's ships. These agreements were irritating and embarrassing for powerful countries because they were forced to submit to the outlaw pirates. Nevertheless, most countries paid the tribute.

The United States at first followed the example of the European countries. Before gaining independence from England, the colonies had been protected under Britain's pact with the pirates. During the American Revolution, American ships relied on the 1778

The USS Constitution, *shown here, was built to fight in the First Barbary War. It is the world's oldest naval vessel still afloat and can be toured in Boston, Massachusetts.*

Treaty of Alliance with France, which required that France protect them. That alliance ended in 1783, however. U.S. officials then negotiated a treaty with the bey, or ruler, of Morocco in 1786, but pirates from Algiers and other provinces still demanded tribute.

When Thomas Jefferson became president in 1801, he refused a demand for increased tribute from the bey of Tripoli. Tripoli responded by declaring war on the United States. Jefferson informed Congress in his inaugural message on December 8, 1801: "Tripoli, the least considerable of the Barbary States ... has permitted itself to denounce war, on our failure to comply before a given day. The style of the demand admitted but one answer. I sent a small squadron of frigates [warships] into the Mediterranean ... with orders to protect our commerce."[13] The announcement marked the start of the First Barbary War.

Two Wars

The First Barbary War, between the United States and Tripoli, lasted from 1801 to 1805. During the war, the United States was successful in defeating Tripoli and raised the U.S. flag in victory on foreign soil for the first time.

The war did not solve the problem of pirate activity in the Mediterranean, however. Algerian privateers in particular continued to capture American ships and hold sailors hostage until ransom was paid. In 1815, the United States once again responded to the attacks in what became known as the Second Barbary War. This short struggle, which lasted from March to July 1815, eventually led to treaties that ended all tribute payments by the United States to the Barbary pirates and gave the United States shipping rights in the Mediterranean.

Beginning in 1816, other European nations also began to resist the demands of the Barbary pirates. With faster ships and increasingly powerful navies, they were better able to win battles in the Mediterranean. Konstam wrote, "The long history of ... piracy ended more with a whimper than a bang, the result of a changing world and the growing importance of military technology."[14] France gained control of Algiers and Tunis and made them colonies in 1830 and 1881 respectively, while Italy assumed control of Tripoli in 1911.

While the corsairs were temporarily defeated in the Mediterranean, other pirates and privateers were still at large in other parts of the world, particularly in the Caribbean Sea. Whether they were called buccaneers or roundsmen, these men (and sometimes women) from Britain, France, and the Netherlands spent years plundering the New World and gained infamy for doing so. Earle wrote, "The pirates of the Americas, who flourished from the 1650s to the 1720s, were ... the only pirates in history to exhibit those characteristics which we expect 'real' pirates to have. They ... created the modern conception of the pirate."[15]

CHAPTER TWO

THE REAL PIRATES OF THE CARIBBEAN

Thanks to the popularity of movies such as the Pirates of the Caribbean franchise, most people are familiar with the basic details of piracy in this part of the world. Some information has been invented or exaggerated, however, and other details have been left out completely. The stories of real pirates are often even more fascinating than the movies about them.

The Caribbean had come under Spanish influence when Christopher Columbus made his voyages to the New World beginning in 1492. In 1521, Spanish explorer Hernán Cortés conquered the Aztec Empire in Mexico and began sending treasure that included exotic animals, enameled gold and jade ornaments, emeralds, pearls, works of art, and mosaic masks back to his country. The rest of Europe learned of those riches when, in 1522, French privateer Jean Fleury captured Spanish ships that were carrying treasure. Author Rene Chartrand wrote, "The news spread like wildfire: the fabulous wealth of the Spanish 'Indies' was soon the envy of all Europe."[16]

Government-Sponsored Piracy

The Spanish Main is a historical term. According to the *Encyclopedia Britannica*,

The term refers to an area that was once under Spanish control and spanned roughly between the Isthmus of Panama and the delta of the Orinoco River. The term can also refer to the Caribbean Sea and adjacent waters, especially when referring to the period when the region was troubled by pirates.[17]

The Spanish Main was a source of enormous wealth for Spain for many years. That wealth created jealousy among other European rulers who wanted to take part in trade and colonization in the New World. Spain,

This map shows the general location of the Spanish Main.

however, was determined to keep the land and riches for itself. As a result, Britain, the Netherlands, France, and Portugal began hiring privateers to attack Spanish ships and landholdings and to steal treasure.

Some of the first privateers to attack Spanish ships were French, including Fleury and François Le Clerc. It is not known exactly when either man began his pirating career, but by 1553, Le Clerc had assumed overall command of seven pirate craft and three royal vessels and was leading major raids against the Spanish, using the island of Saint Lucia as his home base. He was nicknamed Peg Leg by the Spanish because he was missing one leg and had replaced it with a wooden one. Although many pirates in popular fiction have peg legs, eye patches, or hooks for hands, this was not common in real life. Le Clerc may be where the idea of pirates with peg legs came from, although this is not known for certain.

Jacques de Sores, nicknamed the Exterminating Angel, was a lesser-known French privateer who sailed with Le

by kidnapping and ransoming important townspeople. All that is known for certain is he set the town on fire and his attack, which was accomplished easily, encouraged the Spanish government to make its defenses stronger. This uncertainty shows why it is frequently difficult to get accurate accounts of historical piracy.

A Famous Privateer

English privateers also sailed in the Caribbean. They were motivated by a desire for loot but also by a hatred of the Spanish, with whom Britain was at war until the Treaty of London was signed in 1604. The most famous privateer was Sir Francis Drake, whom Queen

Although pirates are often shown in fiction with replacements for missing body parts, there is no evidence that this was common.

Clerc. Almost the only thing known about him is his attack on Havana, Cuba, in 1555. However, the details of the attack are also uncertain and vary in places, sometimes by quite a bit. For instance, some say he attacked with two ships, while others say it was twenty. Some believe he was hoping to find gold on the island, while others say he expected to make money

Elizabeth I called "my pirate."[18] Unlike the French and Barbary corsairs, much is known about him. He came from a family of merchants and privateers, so he started sailing when he was only 18. Within a few years, he had already earned control of his own ship. He used it to work with his cousin, John Hawkins, illegally transporting slaves from Africa to Spain. Commissioned by the queen in 1572, Drake's first official act was to attack the Spanish-owned town of Nombre de Dios in Panama. The town was successfully captured, and although Drake did not find much treasure there, he did get a lot of gold and silver from other nearby towns, so the trip was considered a success.

Drake's piracy extended outside of the Caribbean as well. In 1577, he was secretly commissioned by Elizabeth to undertake an expedition against the Spanish colonies on the Pacific coast of North America. He sailed with five ships, but by the time he rounded the tip of South America and reached the Pacific Ocean in October 1578, only one, a galleon (a large, multi-deck sailing ship) named the *Golden Hind*, remained. He continued up the coast, plundering ships along the way. From one vessel alone, the *Nuestra Señora de la Concepción*, he was able to take silver and gold worth millions in today's dollars. It was one of the most profitable pirate attacks in history. After claiming a portion of California for the queen, Drake continued homeward across the Pacific, making multiple stops as he went, and arriving in Plymouth, England, in July 1580. He was the first Englishman to circumnavigate the globe, a term that describes sailing all the way around the world. In 1588, after a successful fight with a fleet of Spanish ships, he was appointed vice admiral of the British navy.

Drake continued his seafaring career, but on a trip to the Caribbean in 1596, he developed dysentery and died. He was buried at sea off the coast of Panama in a lead coffin, which has never

Sir Francis Drake is one of history's most famous privateers.

been found, although people continue to look for it to this day.

Despite Spanish opposition, countries such as Britain, France, and the Netherlands established colonies in the Spanish Main as well. The British colonized Bermuda in 1612 and Jamaica in 1655. The Dutch took over the islands known as the Dutch West Indies (Aruba, St. Croix, St. Martin, and others) beginning in the 1620s.

French colonization began in 1625 on the island of Hispaniola (now Haiti and the Dominican Republic), which was wild and undeveloped. The Spanish had unsuccessfully tried ranching there, and herds of semi-wild cattle still roamed freely. These cattle became a source of food for the colonists, who survived by smoking meat over a boucan, which was a type of grill. Because of their cooking method, these men became known as boucaniers, which later turned into the word "buccaneers." According to author Philip Gosse, the difference between a pirate and a buccaneer was that a pirate "was a criminal who robbed the ships of all nations in any waters, but the original buccaneer preyed only upon Spanish ships and property in America."[19] Gosse stated that the main reason men became buccaneers was that the Spanish did not provide enough supplies to their colonists. What little they did provide was sold at prices many people could

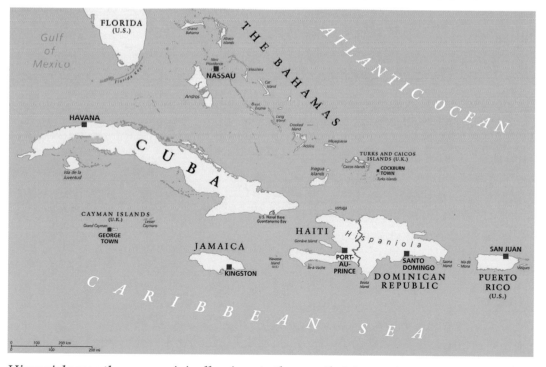

Hispaniola was the name originally given to the area that is now two separate countries: Haiti and the Dominican Republic.

NOT ALL PIRATES WERE WHITE

Better accounts of pirates exist for the Golden Age of Piracy than for any earlier period, but there are no records of the number of black pirates who sailed the Spanish Main. Former librarian Cindy Vallar explained:

> Some estimate that nearly 5,000 pirates hunted prey between 1715 and 1726. Of that number, about twenty-five to thirty percent came from the cimarrons, black slaves who ran from their Spanish masters ...

> Blacks became pirates for the same reasons as other men did, but they also sought the freedom often denied them elsewhere. W. Jeffrey Bolster wrote in Black Jacks, "No accurate numbers of black buccaneers exist, although the impression is that they were more numerous than the proportion of black sailors in commercial or naval service at that time." It isn't known how many of the estimated 400 pirates hanged for their crimes between 1716 and 1726 were black, for the historical record fails to show this. Like their brethren who weren't given the chance to stand trial, but were sold into slavery, these pirates remain lost to history.[1]

1. Cindy Vallar, "Black Pirates," *Pirates and Privateers: The History of Maritime Piracy*, accessed November 29, 2017. www.cindyvallar.com/blackpirates.html.

not afford. This led people of all nationalities who were living in the Spanish colonies to turn to piracy as a way to survive.

Buccaneers included former slaves, indentured servants, and outlaws from America and other parts of the Caribbean. They were also joined by men who had served in the British Royal Navy. From the 1600s to the 1800s, England could impress, or kidnap, any man it wanted and force him to serve on a merchant ship or in the navy. The service was incredibly hard, the wages were low, and the captain of a ship had absolute power. Life was restrictive, and crewmen could be punished by whipping for the least offense. To these men, being a pirate was a vast improvement in lifestyle, as pirate Bartholomew Roberts, otherwise known as Black Bart, testified: "In an honest Service there is thin Commons [limited food], low Wages, and hard Labour; in this [being a pirate], Plenty and Satiety [satisfaction], Pleasure and Ease, Liberty and Power ... A merry Life and a short one, shall be my Motto."[20]

Although most buccaneers were men, there was at least one notable exception. Jacquotte Delahaye was the daughter of a French father and a Haitian mother, both of whom died when she was young. To support herself and her younger brother, Delahaye turned to piracy. She was so successful that she became the target of law enforcement, so she faked her death and reportedly disguised herself as a man until the danger passed. This, combined with her red hair, earned her the nickname Back from the Dead Red.

The Golden Age of Piracy

The activities of the buccaneers between 1650 and 1680 marked the first phase of the Golden Age of Piracy. Today, when people think of piracy, they are often thinking of this time period. Despite Spain's attempts to end piracy, the practice flourished during these years. When authorities tried to clear Hispaniola of the buccaneers, they moved to the nearby island of Tortuga. The island was small—only about 20 miles long and 4 miles wide (32 km by 6.4 km)—but it had fresh water and good anchorage for ships. Over the years, it had been fought over by the Spanish, Dutch, French, and English. After the buccaneers first claimed it around 1630, they were driven off by the Spanish. However, in 1640, a French former engineer named Jean Le Vasseur gathered together 50 Frenchmen and launched a surprise attack on Tortuga, successfully claiming it for the pirates.

Le Vasseur became the governor of this pirate town.

Le Vasseur used his training to build a large, heavily armed fort by the harbor, which kept the Spanish away. He also welcomed any outlaw to the island as long as Le Vasseur was given a share of the man's plunder. By 1650, Tortuga was one of the primary pirate strongholds in the Caribbean, and it grew rich. Buccaneers planted crops such as tobacco and sugar there, and meat was available because people hunted the wild cattle on Hispaniola. Additionally, many pirates came to trade things from around the world and get rich by plundering Spanish ships. As Gosse described it:

> Tortuga soon became the mart for the boucan and hides brought from Hispaniola, and for plunder taken from the Spanish, which were bartered for brandy, guns, gunpowder and cloth from the Dutch and French ships which called there.
>
> It was not long before the fame of Tortuga had spread all over the West Indies, to be followed by a rush of adventurers of all kinds, to whom the attraction of cruising after the Spaniards with its opportunities of sudden wealth was irresistible.[21]

Tortuga was not the only pirate haven in the Caribbean. On the island of Jamaica, English governors Edward D'Oyley and Thomas Modyford

Tortuga, shown here, was a famous pirate base during the Golden Age of Piracy.

granted letters of marque—documents that gave people official government sponsorship—to anyone who wanted to harass and plunder Spanish ships. The English privateers also attacked Spanish-held towns such as Tolú in Colombia and Portobelo in Panama. Earle wrote, "In the sixteen years following the English conquest of Jamaica in 1655, the privateers and flibustiers sacked eighteen cities, four towns and over thirty-five villages ... Some places were raided time and time again ... and smaller villages and settlements on the south coasts of Cuba and Hispaniola were ravaged even more often."[22]

Another Pirate Stronghold

On Jamaica, Port Royal was the spot where pirates gathered to do business and have fun. A city of 6,500, its citizens tolerated piracy because they profited from it. The harbor held hundreds of ships, from narrow-hulled, shallow-drafted schooners to larger galleons and captured merchant ships. Warehouses held stolen merchandise. Plundered gold and silver flowed into the city. Konstam wrote, "In its heyday [best days] Port Royal was larger and more prosperous than any other city in the Americas, apart from Boston."[23]

Known as the Wickedest City on Earth, the settlement also had plenty of taverns, gambling dens, and brothels, or houses of prostitution. In July 1661, for instance, 40 new licenses were granted for taverns in the city, and it has been estimated by historians that one in every four buildings was a bar or a brothel. One minister who arrived, planning to attend to the spiritual needs of the inhabitants, immediately left on the same ship, saying that "since the majority of its population consists of pirates, cutthroats, [prostitutes] and some of the vilest persons in the whole of the world, I felt my permanence [staying] there was of no use."[24]

Port Royal's glory was short-lived. On the morning of June 7, 1692, a massive earthquake hit the island. The tremors rocked the sandy peninsula on which the town was built, causing buildings to slide and disappear beneath the sea. An estimated 2,000 townspeople were killed immediately in the disaster. Many more died from injuries and disease in the following days. Some survivors, such as Anglican priest Emmanuel Heath, saw the earthquake as a sign of God's wrath and hoped that the disaster would change Port Royalists' behavior. "By this terrible Judgment," Heath stated, "God will make them reform their lives, for there was not a more ungodly People on the Face of the Earth."[25]

Today, Port Royal still exists, although it is no longer a pirate base. In 2012, BBC News reported that

Pirates went to Port Royal to drink and gamble. Popular methods of gambling included dice and card games.

HOW PIRATES GOT THEIR SHIPS

Pirates always needed good ships in which to sail, but they did not buy and sell them like ordinary people would. Author David Cordingly explained in *Under the Black Flag*:

> Unlike the Royal Navy or the East India Company or the merchants of London or Boston, the pirates could not build a ship to order. They could only acquire vessels which came their way ... The majority of pirate ships were prizes, ships captured by force. Operating outside the law, the pirates could not ... go along to the prize courts to get their captured vessels valued and sold, which was the usual practice of privateer captains. Having looted a ship, the pirates would burn the vessel or set her adrift. However, if the pirate captain liked the look of the ship, he would either take her over for his own use or employ her as a consort [a member of his fleet].[1]

1. David Cordingly, *Under the Black Flag: The Romance and the Reality of Life Among the Pirates*. New York, NY: Random House, 1995, p. 160.

archaeologists are working to uncover the old buildings and pirate ships, which are preserved underwater. Journalist Nick Davis wrote, "It is one of the most important underwater sites in the world, according to Robert Grenier, a Canadian marine archaeologist."[26] Many historians as well as Port Royal residents hope the past can be uncovered and restored. In addition to being a major archaeological find, restoring the old pirate town might boost Jamaica's economy by bringing in tourists.

An Unstoppable Force

Not even an earthquake stopped the pirates of the Caribbean, who became known as the Brethren of the Coast. Based out of Port Royal and Tortuga, they attacked Spanish merchant ships, using small sailing or rowing boats called pinnaces and single-masted boats called sloops. These light vessels allowed the pirates to hide in the shallow waters of small bays and inlets and wait for their prey, then maneuver quickly up to a larger ship and attack.

The most famous of this group was Henry Morgan. Morgan was born in Wales, part of the United Kingdom, in 1635. According to *Encyclopedia Britannica*,

Morgan's origins and early career are obscure. He was probably a member of the expedition that in 1655 seized Jamaica from the Spanish and converted it into an English colony. He may have participated in an expedition against Cuba in 1662; and, during the second Anglo-Dutch War (1665–67), he was second in command of the buccaneers operating against Dutch colonies in the Caribbean.[27]

In 1668, after becoming the leader of the Caribbean buccaneers, Morgan captured Puerto Principe, Cuba, with only 10 ships and 500 men. He then went on to take the fortified and well-protected town of Portobelo, Panama, which was guarded by three forts, all of which Morgan and his men conquered. He returned to Port Royal with a massive amount of treasure, which gave him a good reputation with Governor Modyford. In 1669, assigned to attack the Spanish along the coast of Venezuela, Morgan made a successful raid on the Lake Maracaibo region, returning to Port Royal with another boatload of treasure.

In 1670, Morgan embarked on the most daring adventure of his career with 36 ships and 2,000 men: the capture of the city of Panama. The city was a stopover point on the overland route where gold and silver from the Incan Empire were transported from Peru to the Atlantic coast. At the time, there was no Panama Canal, so access to the city was difficult, and Morgan's band had to cross mountains and push through thick jungle to get there. After the difficult trek and several battles, the pirates succeeded in taking the city, which was burned in the process.

Although Morgan's raid was successful, it was completed after England and Spain had signed a peace treaty, so his actions were no longer protected by the British government. When Panama

Captain Henry Morgan's name is still recognized today, although not all stories about him are true.

AN EXAGGERATED REPUTATION

Henry Morgan had a reputation for being bloodthirsty and violent, but many believe this was invented and spread in a book. The title of the book and the identity of its author vary; according to Gosse, it was written by the buccaneers' "own historian, Alexander Olivier Exquemelin, or Esquemeling, a young Frenchman."[1] Other accounts say his name was John and that he was Dutch or Flemish. It was published in Dutch in 1678 as *The Buccaneers of America* and reprinted in English, Spanish, and French as *The History of the Buccaneers of America*. Today, it can be found under both titles. Exquemelin was, by some accounts, one of Morgan's crewmates, and his book is classified as nonfiction. Both of these facts may explain why the book was so popular and widely believed.

Exquemelin told stories that made Morgan sound like a monster. For example, he wrote that Morgan forced nuns and priests to act as human shields when Morgan conquered the third fort at Portobelo and that he and his crew spent five weeks torturing prisoners after conquering Lake Maracaibo. Morgan's official reports contradicted these stories. He was so outraged by the book that he sued the English publishers and was awarded a large amount of money as well as a public apology. However, the book remained popular and is still reprinted today, often without the apology. It has been said to be one of the most comprehensive accounts of pirate life during the Golden Age, and much of what is currently known about pirates has come from it, although it is uncertain how much is true.

1. Philip Gosse, *The History of Piracy*. New York, NY: Longmans, Green and Co., 1932, p. 145.

complained to England, Morgan was arrested and sent to London in 1672. However, peace between the two countries did not last long, so King Charles II pardoned and knighted Morgan in 1674. He became the assistant governor of Jamaica, "where he lived as a wealthy and respected planter until his death"[28] in 1688.

Searching for Treasure

The second part of the Golden Age of Piracy began in the 1690s. It was characterized by long ocean voyages that started from the Caribbean and launched out into the Atlantic and beyond to the Indian Ocean. When enough ships had been attacked and enough treasure taken, the pirates would sail back to their home port. These excursions were known as the Pirate Round, and those who made them discovered, in the words of Konstam, "[the Indian Ocean was] a pirate's dream—rich and poorly protected prizes … the most lucrative pirate destination in the world."[29]

There were several reasons why some pirates went on these rounds, looking beyond the Caribbean for riches. First, by the 1690s, the largest reserves of treasure had been taken from the region. Second, the devastation of Port Royal destroyed one of their chief markets for stolen goods. Third, it was from India that high-value luxury goods such as silk, spices, and jewels were being transported to Europe. Fourth, while pirate attacks were expected in the Spanish Main and ships that sailed there were becoming more protected,

no powerful navies operated in the waters of the Indian Ocean, so the enormous merchant ships that sailed there were open to attack and capture. The area was too tempting for adventurous men to ignore.

American Thomas Tew, also known as the Rhode Island Pirate, was the first to make the Pirate Round. He traveled from the United States to Bermuda in 1691 to buy a share of a ship called the *Amity*. He was appointed captain of the ship, and he and his crew set sail to the Indian Ocean and the Red Sea. In the Red Sea in 1693, he successfully captured a warship owned by the Indian emperor Alamgir I that carried a fortune in coins, jewels, ivory, spices, and silks. When he returned to America with the treasure, he became a hero to men such

This pirate chest is the only known authentic pirate chest in America. It belonged to Thomas Tew and can be viewed at the Pirate Soul Museum in Key West, Florida.

as Governor Benjamin Fletcher of New York, who enjoyed the friendship of pirates and accepted gifts from them. Tew was not successful for long, however. On his second voyage, in September 1694, he and his crew were pursuing a convoy of merchant ships in the Red Sea when he was wounded. He died from his injuries; his final resting place is unknown.

Madagascar: A Pirate Base

After Tew, other pirates began making the Pirate Round. They generally set off across the Atlantic to the coast of Africa, sailed around the Cape of Good Hope, and then stopped at the island of Madagascar, where they could get fresh provisions and clean their ship's hulls. After being at sea for months, hulls collected barnacles, weeds, and infestations of worms, which slowed ships down and damaged them.

The island was perfect for a stopover. It was close to trading routes and had plenty of coves where, at low tide, repairs could be made. The small bands of native people who lived there did not mind pirates coming to their shores. Antongil Bay on the northern edge of Madagascar and Nosy

Boraha, also called St. Mary's Island, a small island off the northeast coast, were both used as bases for attacking passing merchant ships. The island was so inviting that many pirates remained there, becoming pirate "kings" rather than going back to the Caribbean. For instance, pirate Abraham Samuel set up a business as a trader on the island around 1696 and called himself the King of Port Dolphin. Another former pirate, James Plantain, was known as the King of Ranter's Bay.

Once pirates left Madagascar, the next leg of the Pirate Round was where most of the actual piracy took place. In the Persian Gulf, the Red Sea, and the Indian Ocean, the pirates attacked merchant ships, particularly the large and

The Pirate Round involved long stretches of time on the open sea.

heavily loaded East Indiamen. These ships were specially designed to hold passengers and cargo and were operated under charter, or license, to any of the East India Companies of the major European trading powers. Because the Indiamen were fitted with cannons and had plenty of storage facilities, the pirates often kept these ships as their own for the rest of the Round. At other times, the captured ships were sailed into port and sold. No matter what the decision, once the pirates were satisfied with their loot, they turned and sailed back across the Atlantic, sometimes stopping again in Madagascar to refit their ships or wait for favorable winds.

Piracy on the Red Sea

Roundsmen, also known as Red Sea Men, were legendary for the riches they captured. Henry Every, also called John Avery or Long Ben, became known for capturing a ship personally owned by Emperor Aurangzeb of India. The ship was not only heavily armed and guarded, it also held millions of dollars worth of gold. In response to his attack on the ship, the Indian emperor ordered the East India Company, which was owned by the British government, to close some of its Indian trading posts. This made the company so angry at Every that it offered a large reward for his capture, which led to the first worldwide manhunt in history. Nevertheless, Every managed to escape his hunters. What happened to him is not known for certain. By some accounts, he simply

disappeared in 1696; others say he lived in Northern Ireland and tried to sell his treasure but was cheated by the merchants he talked to, who took his gems and never sent him the money they promised to pay him. In this version, Every became ill and died in poverty. In either case, he was one of the few major pirate captains to have escaped arrest or death in battle.

Scottish pirate William Kidd, commonly known as Captain Kidd, was another famous Roundsman. Kidd began his career as a privateer for the British, then was commissioned in 1696 by Massachusetts royal governor Richard Coote to become a pirate hunter. However, as Kidd sailed for the Indian Ocean in his ship, the *Adventure Galley*, he had a change of heart and instead of catching pirates, he became one himself.

Kidd pirated for nearly three years before he met his fate. When Kidd and his crew learned they were wanted criminals, they sailed back to America and Kidd turned himself in to the governor of Boston, hoping to gain a pardon. Instead, he was arrested and sent to London. There he was put on trial and found guilty of piracy and the murder of one of his crewmen, William Moore, whom he had smashed over the head with a wooden bucket in a fit of rage in 1697.

Joining Forces

The third phase of the Golden Age of Piracy began around 1716 and lasted until about 1726. It was characterized by a combination of piracy from the two earlier periods—plundering in the Caribbean and treasure hunting in the Indian Ocean. Shipping between Africa, the Caribbean, and Europe soared in the 1700s, providing more targets for pirates to prey upon. The end of the War of the Spanish Succession, which had involved Spain, Britain, and other European countries and had lasted from 1701 to 1714, meant that many sailors were idle and looking for work. They formed a pool of experienced men who saw piracy as a way to make a living. About 2,000 pirates in some 25 to 30 ships were on the seas during this active period of pirate history.

With so many pirates on the high seas, their crimes made news both in America and Europe. Newspaper accounts warned merchants and passengers of the danger and provided fascinating tales of the outlaws' activities. These tales were often so dramatic that they were hard to believe. However, they are the best resource historians currently have about the lives of these pirates.

CHAPTER THREE

PIRATE CULTURE

Much remains unknown about pirate life. Although several books were written by pirates that described their activities during the Golden Age of Piracy, some of these accounts are not verifiable. Certain things, such as Henry Morgan's violent reputation, have been denounced as false, which sheds doubt on the rest of what is written. However, they are still the best sources historians have about pirate life, and it is unlikely that everything is false.

In 1724, a book called *A General History of the Robberies and Murders of the Most Notorious Pyrates*, later shortened to *A General History of the Pyrates*, was published and included a great deal of information, some of which came from the pirates themselves. The name of the author, Captain Charles Johnson, was fictitious, but many guessed

Many people are certain Charles Johnson was actually famous author Daniel Defoe (shown here), but there is no way to know for sure.

that he had been either a pirate or author Daniel Defoe, who had much knowledge of pirates and the sea. In fact, the book has been reprinted with Defoe, rather than Johnson, given credit as the author, even though it has not been proven that he wrote it. Some believe the author was a man named Woodes Rogers, a privateer who later became a pirate hunter, or journalist Nathaniel Mist. Author David Cordingly wrote, "Whatever the identity of the author, the book has had a far-reaching effect on popular views of pirates."[30] Devin Leigh, a history PhD candidate at the University of California, Davis, noted that the book

> is largely responsible for setting down our popular imagery concerning pirates of the early-modern era. For example, although many literary scholars attribute the idea of burying gold to the eighteenth-century Scottish novelist Robert Louis Stevenson, it was Charles Johnson who claimed that [pirate Edward] Teach said, "no body but himself, and the Devil, know where" he "buried his money."[31]

Choosing Freedom and Equality

Details of pirates' lives revealed their desire for freedom and their rejection of rank and authority. All were rebellious of the rules and regulations of society. Many had criminal pasts, so they kept the details of their former lives hidden. As Earle wrote, "Buccaneers were so determined to forget the social hierarchy of the outside world that it was forbidden to speak of a man's origins, and surnames which might have given those origins away were replaced by noms de guerre [names of war] or nicknames."[32]

Many men, especially Englishmen, became pirates to escape the British navy, which had a tendency to kidnap men to make up their crews. The hours were long, the work was hard, and the pay was very low. When the ships docked, men who had not volunteered to be in the navy were locked up so they could not escape. According to Cindy Vallar,

> Seamen, whether pressed [forced] or not, found life aboard ships of the Royal Navy deplorable ... Corruption impacted the quantity and quality of food served them. Mistakes or infractions were countered with violent discipline. Poor ventilation and cramped quarters ensured that epidemics swept through the crew, killing many.[33]

In contrast to the navy, life aboard pirate ships was based on democracy at a time when few democracies existed in the world. Instead of being ordered around by a superior officer, all crew members had equal voting rights on important issues. Pirate crews had a say in the division of treasure, in compensation for the injured, and in rules of behavior. No one had better or more food than anyone else, and punishments for misbehavior were equal as well, even for the captain. According to author Brenda Ralph Lewis, "The Quartermaster, who was in charge of discipline onboard and thus the real master of a pirate ship, was elected by the pirate crew as was, sometimes, the captain."[34]

One of the best known sets of articles was created in 1720 by Bartholomew Roberts, also known as Black Bart, and his men. Some of their rules seem astonishing for their strictness and respectability. They set hours at which lights had to be put out—8:00 p.m. They prohibited gambling for money on board, taking women on board, and fighting on board. Some pirate codes also specified how much money a man would receive if he lost an appendage, such as a hand, or a limb, such as an arm.

Some pirates had a custom called *matelotage*, which was an agreement between two men where if something happened to one of them, the other would inherit his possessions and property. It is believed this is why pirates called each other "matey." Some people have said this was a homosexual relationship similar to a civil marriage; however, many historians have pointed out that this is not consistent with attitudes toward homosexuality in the 16th and 17th centuries. Although pirates were more democratic than the navy, there is no evidence that they were more tolerant of homosexuality. Because they spent long stretches at sea and no women were allowed on most ships, it can safely be assumed that some homosexual activity took place, but the available evidence shows that this was generally frowned upon. For instance, in the rules set down by the Brethren of the Coast, it was stated that any man who tried to start a relationship with a male crewmate would be punished, and if two men kept a relationship secret, they would be marooned.

Honor Among Thieves

It was standard for most articles, including Roberts's, to state that every pirate was to have a vote on important decisions. Each was to get an equal share of any treasure that was captured, although the captain and quartermaster generally received two shares. The quartermaster ranked higher than other ship officers because in addition to being responsible for discipline, he also led the pirate boarding party when it invaded another ship. Pirates were not generally required to remain on a ship for any set length of time; they could come and go as they pleased.

Marooned pirates were left on uninhabited islands.

Still, they had no right to desert or disobey the captain during battle. Roberts's rules stated, "To Desert the Ship, or their Quarters in Battle, was punished with Death, or Marooning."[35] Marooning involved leaving someone on an uninhabited island to survive as best he could.

Stealing from shipmates and having sex with a woman without her consent were also punishable by marooning or death. Some rules carried lesser punishments. For example, smoking on the ship or carrying a lit candle—both things that could set the ship on fire if they were not done properly—were punishable by whipping. Many pirates broke the rules, but the guidelines helped keep order among those who had to live in close quarters for long periods of time. As one pirate who sailed under Captain Edward Low admitted, "If we once take the liberty of breaking our articles and oath, then there is none of us can be sure of anything."[36]

The Pirate Life

Pirate ships were crowded places because they had so many men aboard. Merchant ships commonly had a crew of 10 to 18, but a pirate crew could include up to 300. The numbers were higher for several reasons. First, there were a large number of guns that needed to be manned on pirate vessels. Also, when attacks were made, a large number of pirates were needed to swarm onto the victim ship and overcome any resistance.

The average age of a pirate was 27; young men were more willing to put up with the discomfort of all kinds of weather they encountered at sea. Youthfulness was also a necessity because of the physical demands of working on a ship. This included hoisting sails and hauling on ropes, as well as climbing the rigging and carrying heavy cargo.

Music helped make the hard work easier, so musicians, commonly fiddlers and accordion players, were especially valued on board a pirate ship. Musicians provided accompaniment to sea shanties, songs that pirates sang to help synchronize their movements as they performed tasks. For instance, halyard shanties were sung while the sails were raised or lowered. Windlass shanties accompanied raising the anchor. Pumping shanties attended pumping water out of the bilge, the lowest part of the ship.

In addition to musicians, other members of the crew were valued for their special expertise. For instance, every ship needed a doctor on board. If one did not come willingly, a doctor might be kidnapped and taken to sea against his will. Several men needed to be skilled at carpentry, both to make repairs and to do remodeling. When a merchant ship was captured and the crew members chose to take it as one of their own, carpenters were able to refit it quickly with extra guns and remove parts to make it lighter and faster.

Although some pirates had specific skills, most were poor, uneducated men. Captain Stede Bonnet was one exception. Bonnet was known as the Gentleman Pirate because he was the son of a wealthy English landowner who lived on the island of Barbados. In 1717, perhaps because he was bored or unhappy with his ordinary life or, as some historians believe, because of a mental breakdown caused in part by financial problems, he left his land and his wife behind and purchased a sloop that he named the *Revenge*. He then began attacking and plundering ships along the eastern coast of North America.

Bonnet met up with Edward Teach, better known as the pirate Blackbeard, and the two agreed to sail side by side. However, Blackbeard quickly realized that Bonnet had almost no sailing experience, so it was easy for him to seize Bonnet's ship. Eventually he abandoned it, and Bonnet was able to take it back. According to *Smithsonian* magazine, he built a reputation for himself by "abusing his crew, killing prisoners and threatening civilians."[37] In 1718, he and his

Stede Bonnet (pictured here) left his life as a gentleman and took up pirating even though he had little sailing experience. He learned over time and eventually made a name for himself.

will be needless for me to explain to you the Nature of Repentance."[38] Bonnet blamed most of his crimes on Blackbeard, but this did not work: He was hanged in December 1718 on the waterfront of Charleston, South Carolina.

Women Who Went to Sea

Another pirate who died by hanging was John "Calico Jack" Rackham, captain of the *William*. Rackham was noteworthy because two members of his crew were female. Women in piracy were rare in Europe and America. They were seen as distractions and as agents of bad luck. Rackham apparently did not worry about those potential problems. In 1719, while in the Bahamas, he met and began

crew were captured by South Carolina governor William Rhett. They were tried and found guilty, and the judge emphasized Bonnet's educated background when he pronounced his sentence: "Major Stede Bonnet, you stand here convict'd on 2 indictments of Pyracy … You being a Gentleman that have had the advantage of a liberal education, and being generally esteemed a Man of Letters, I believe it

a relationship with an Irish woman named Anne Bonny, wife of James Bonny, a former pirate turned informant for the British government. Anne left her husband, put on men's clothes, and went off to pirate with Rackham. Her shipmates knew she was a woman, but when she joined raiding parties, she disguised herself as a man. Johnson wrote, "Anne Bonny kept him company, and when

It is unknown how many women were pirates during the Golden Age of Piracy. Anne Bonny and Mary Read (pictured here) are the two most famous of this era.

any business was to be done in their way, nobody was more forward or courageous than she."[39]

At some point when Bonny and Rackham were sailing together, another interesting newcomer joined their crew. She was an Englishwoman named Mary Read, also disguised as a man. Read had dressed as a boy in her youth and was used to passing as a man. Both she and Bonny remained with Rackham and proved to be extremely good at pirating, even taking part in battles with men. According to Johnson, "In times of action, no Person amongst

them was more resolute, or ready to Board or undertake any Thing that was hazardous."[40]

In 1720, Rackham's ship was attacked and captured by an armed sloop sent by Jamaican authorities. The women were the only ones on the ship who were not too drunk to put up a fight. Rackham and his crew were taken to Jamaica, where they were tried and sentenced to be hanged. The men's sentences were carried out right away, but both women claimed to be pregnant, so they were given a stay of execution until they gave birth. Read died in

AN OPPORTUNITY FOR WOMEN

Many women went into piracy for the same reasons no matter where they were from. Author Cathy Converse explained in "The Lady Was a Pirate":

There are various reasons why women chose to become pirates. Many women were connected with male pirate leaders, working on their father's, husband's or lover's ship or were pushed into it by unscrupulous men. In most cases piracy seemed the best available option for them. Usually women pirates came from poverty stricken circumstances where prostitution or low-waged personal service was a more common route for industrious women to survive. Given access to ships and the sea, contacts and opportunity, some women chose a life of piracy instead. And why not, they reasoned, for with few exceptions each pirate received an equal share of the spoils [treasure], the food was better and life in general was more comfortable. They became self-sufficient and depended on no man nor fickle social circumstance for survival. The life of a pirate offered women extraordinary mobility, with the chance of doing well financially—for Cheng I Sao [Zheng Yi Sao] it was total control over the China merchant trade.[1]

1. Cathy Converse, "The Lady Was a Pirate," The Nautical Institute. www.nauticalinstitute. ca/Articles/files/lady_pirate.htm.

prison in April 1721, but Bonny was for some reason spared execution and released. Before Rackham was executed on November 18, 1720, he got special permission to see Bonny, but she did not offer much comfort. She stated she was "sorry to see him there [in prison], but if he had fought like a Man, he need not have been hang'd like a Dog."[41]

Although Bonny and Read are two of the most famous female pirates, they were not the first. Teuta of Illyria was a pirate queen who ruled over the Ardiaei tribe of what is now the Western Balkans. She led her subjects in plundering Roman ships until the loss of a war with Rome forced her to give up her throne. Another pirate queen ruled during the time of the Barbarossa brothers. Her real name is unknown; she was called Sayyida al Hurra, a title that reportedly means "noble lady who is free and independent; the woman sovereign who bows to no superior authority."[42] She ruled the eastern Mediterranean Sea while the Barbarossa brothers ruled the western side. At one point, she married the king of Morocco, which doubled her power, making her queen of both Morocco and the pirate city of Tétouan until her son-in-law overthrew her in 1542.

One of the most feared pirates in history was a Chinese woman. According to the History Channel, her birth name is unknown, although some claim it is Shi Xiang Gu. She was working as a prostitute in China when she was captured by pirates. She married the pirate Zheng Yi in 1801, and when he died, she changed her name to Zheng Yi Sao—sometimes written Ching Shih—and took over his fleet. According to the website Mental Floss,

> To help her maintain the day-to-day concerns of a sprawling pirate army, Ching Shih enlisted the help of Chang Pao, a fisherman's son who had been adopted by Yi. They proved a great team, and by 1810 the Red Fleet is said to have grown to 1800 sailing vessels and 80,000 crew members. To manage so many, Ching Shih essentially set up her own government to establish laws and even taxes. Yet she was no soft touch. Breaking her laws [led] to decapitation. She was revered [respected] and feared as far away as Great Britain.[43]

She retired honorably from piracy when amnesty—forgiveness of crimes by the government—was offered in 1810. She was one of the only pirates in history to keep her honor, her life, and all her treasure.

A Superstitious Bunch

Like Bonny, few pirates would have sympathized with Rackham's death. They would have pointed out that he had brought it about by taking Read and Bonny aboard his ship. Most pirates started out as other kinds of sailors, such as merchants, so sailing superstitions played a large role in pirate life. Pirates, like most sailors, took their superstitions very seriously, even though these beliefs could be contradictory. For instance, a common superstition held that women were bad luck on a ship, while at the same time claiming that the female form could calm a storm at sea. To satisfy such a contradictory view, pirates banned women from their ships but attached a figurehead—a carved shape of a woman to the bow as a good luck piece. These figures were colorfully painted and were generally unclothed from the waist up.

Pirates had other superstitions besides those relating to women. For instance, they preferred not to set sail on Fridays because they believed it was bad luck. This has two sources: In Norse mythology, it was the day evil witches were believed to gather, and in Christian legend, it was the day Jesus was crucified. Sailing on Friday the 13th was doubly unlucky.

Pirates believed manta rays were dangerous.

On the other hand, the 17th and the 29th of any month were considered good days to set sail, particularly if the voyage was going to last many months.

Sharks following in the wake of a ship were thought to be unlucky and meant someone aboard would soon die. Manta rays, also known as devilfish or sea devils, were feared as much as sharks because they were believed to attach themselves to a ship's anchor and drag the ship under the water. Small seabirds known as stormy petrels were good luck because they were supposedly sent from Mary, the mother of Jesus, to warn pirates of coming storms. Tattoos and piercings were good luck as well and may have explained why many pirates were tattooed and wore gold hoop earrings. Another explanation, some say, is that pierced ears were believed to be a cure for seasickness or a way to pay for a pirate's funeral if he died. It is unknown whether these explanations are fact or myth.

A Pirate's Wardrobe

In the days when men traditionally wore dark, formal clothing, including longtailed coats and top hats, pirates were known for their casual, colorful appearance, including their multicolor mix of clothing. Most pirate clothing had a useful purpose. For instance, many pirates wore bandanas on their heads to keep sweat out of their eyes, and sashes or belts were often worn so they could keep their weapons and other tools handy. Some who were British ex-seamen started out in outfits called slops, which consisted of canvas jackets with or without sleeves and breeches that reached the knees. Many pirates also wore knitted caps called Monmouth caps, stockings, and linen shirts. Some wore shoes, but not if this would interfere with their duties. It was easier to grip the wood or rope of a ship with bare feet. This outfit changed as pieces wore out and as pirates picked up replacement apparel. The replacements could include anything from three-cornered hats to buckled shoes and coats with large gold buttons. Pirate clothing tended to be tight because loose-fitting clothing could easily get caught and rip or put the pirate in a dangerous situation where he could not move.

Pirates accessorized themselves with an assortment of weapons,

Pirates are often shown wearing bandanas on their head. These helped keep the sweat out of their eyes.

AN ELEGANT BUT FEARED PIRATE

When it came to appearance, Bartholomew Roberts, who sailed the seas between 1719 and 1722, was considered one of the most elegantly dressed pirates of the Golden Age. Described as a tall, handsome man, he loved expensive clothes and jewelry. During one battle, he wore a crimson vest and a scarlet plumed hat, and on his chest, a massive gold chain with a diamond cross hanging from it.

As unusual as his clothing, Roberts drank tea, forbade gambling, and encouraged prayer on his ship. Still, he was one of the most successful pirates of the Golden Age. He led a fleet of pirate ships that was so menacing that naval ships turned back at the sight of it. He was believed to have captured almost 500 ships during his pirate career.

As with most pirates, Roberts's luck ran out before he grew old. In February 1722, the British government sent a warship and a party of men to find and capture him. During their attack on his ship, the *Royal Fortune*, he was killed. Without their captain, the crew lost its nerve and surrendered, but not before they weighted Roberts's body down and buried it at sea, where it was never found.

especially when an attack was to be made. For instance, Blackbeard went into battle with a short sword called a cutlass, three pairs of pistols strapped across his chest, and daggers and pistols in his belt. Although guns at the time were not as accurate as the guns of today, pirates practiced extensively and were often very accurate. According to Earle, "The buccaneers were able to hit a coin spinning at 120 paces or to sever an orange from a tree by its stalk … They were certainly effective marksmen."[44]

Although pirates are often shown with parrots or monkeys on their shoulders, there are no accounts of pirates keeping these animals as pets.

However, they were known to steal and sell them. Parrots were picked up in exotic ports in South America and Africa and were particularly popular because they could be taught to talk and could be sold for a lot of money or presented to officials as bribes. Pirate William Dampier wrote of the parrots he and his crewmates collected in the West Indies: "There was scarce a man but what sent aboard one or two of them. So that with provision, chests, hen-coops and parrot cages, our ships were full."[45]

The Pirate Flag
When getting ready to attack their victims, pirates hoisted flags on their

ships that were known as Jolly Rogers. Like much else in pirate history, the origin of the name is not known for certain. One theory is that it came from the fact that solid red pirate flags were called *jolie rouge*, or "pretty red," by the French. When people who did not speak French could not pronounce it correctly, it became corrupted, or changed, to Jolly Roger. Another explanation is that it is a corruption of Ali Raja, a title for some Asian pirate captains; a third is that Old Roger, a British nickname for the devil, ended up becoming attached to pirates, who enjoyed causing mischief.

The most famous Jolly Roger has a skull and crossbones on it, but pirates often flew solid red or black flags with no design at all. A black flag indicated that victims could surrender and not be killed, whereas a red one meant that the pirates were going to fight to the death and show no mercy. Captain Richard Hawkins, who was captured by pirates in 1724, reported that "when they fight under Jolly Roger, they give quarter [mercy], which they do not when they fight under the red or bloody flag."[46]

Real flags were distinct to their owner. Blackbeard's flag portrayed a devilish skeleton spearing a red heart. Bartholomew Roberts had two flags. One showed a figure of himself and a skeleton holding an hourglass, and the other showed a figure of himself standing on two skulls. Calico Jack Rackham's flag had a skull and crossed swords.

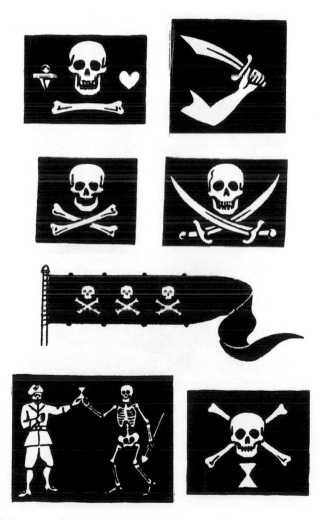

Most people are familiar with the skull-and-crossbones or skull-and-crossed-swords designs of the Jolly Roger, but most pirate flags did not look like that.

Accounts of Violence

According to the firsthand accounts of piracy that are available, real pirates were often cruel cutthroats who tortured, raped, and killed their victims. By modern standards, some would be considered psychopaths—persons who commit antisocial and violent acts and feel no sorrow or guilt for what they have done. However, it is uncertain how accurate these portrayals are. Some stories were likely made up to shock people and sell more books, but others were probably true. Unfortunately, so many years later, it is nearly impossible to tell the difference.

Dutch pirate Roche Brasiliano was one of these most brutal men. He operated in the Caribbean in the 1660s and according to Exquemelin, "He perpetrated the greatest atrocities possible against [his enemies] the Spaniards. Some of them he tied or spitted on wooden stakes and roasted them alive between two fires, like killing a pig."[47] Even while ashore, Brasiliano would reportedly run up and down streets, attacking, beating, and wounding anyone who crossed his path.

Edward Low, who sailed from 1690 to 1724, was also said to have a violent temper and to kill without provocation. For instance, when he became annoyed at the quality of the meals prepared by a captured French ship's cook, he decided that the man was "a greasy fellow, [who] would fry well in the fire."[48] The cook was tied to the main mast and burnt with his ship. When another ship's captain offended Low, he cut off the victim's ears, slit his nose, and hacked up his body. Low was hated and feared but never captured. Johnson observed, "I have heard that he talked of going to Brazil ... though the best information we could receive, would be, that he and all his crew were at the bottom of the sea."[49]

Not all pirates were as cruel as Brasiliano and Low, but torture was regularly used to find out where treasure was hidden, when other ships were sailing, and other valuable information. Common methods of torture and punishment included beating, or flogging, victims; hanging them by their wrists or genitals; marooning them without food or water; or "woolding" them by tightening knotted cords around their head.

Walking the plank is a kind of torture often referred to in fiction, and Johnson wrote about it as well, but according to the History Channel, there is no evidence to suggest that it was actually practiced. Although Johnson's book makes a mention of it, the History Channel's website appears to discount the book as a fictional story written by Defoe.

The Infamous Blackbeard

Edward Teach, or Blackbeard, is one of the most famous pirates to have

In fiction, pirates commonly make prisoners walk the plank, but there is no evidence that real pirates did this often, if they did it at all.

lived. He was born in England and began pirating in the Caribbean in 1717. On his ship *Queen Anne's Revenge*, a former cargo vessel, he led a group of pirates based out of New Providence, an island in the Bahamas.

New Providence was a pirate stronghold between 1715 and 1725, the late part of the Golden Age of Piracy. New Providence easily accommodated hundreds of pirate ships but was too shallow for the larger Royal Navy vessels to enter. British

governor Woodes Rogers helped bring law and order to the Bahamas in 1718, but by then, Blackbeard had moved on and was plundering along the Carolinas.

Although he had a ferocious reputation, Blackbeard never tortured those he held in captivity; according to historian David M. Ullian, there are no trustworthy accounts of Blackbeard even killing anyone. He commanded his ships with the permission of his crews and relied on his fierce looks to terrify his victims and

One of the things Blackbeard was famous for was making his beard smoke to frighten his enemies.

the governor of Charleston, South Carolina, that if the ransom was not paid within two days, the prisoners would be killed and their heads would be cut off and displayed on sticks. Additionally, he said, he would burn every ship in the Charleston harbor. The ransom was paid, so the town never had to find out whether Blackbeard would do as he said.

A tall man, he grew his black hair and beard extremely long and twisted it into ribbons and tails. When going into battle, he stuck lighted matches into his beard on each side of his face so his head was surrounded by smoke. Johnson wrote, "His Eyes, naturally looking Fierce and Wild, made him altogether such a Figure, that Imagination cannot form an idea of a Fury … to look more frightful."[50]

get their cooperation. There are many accounts of his terrible threats, but it seems that people often gave him what he wanted before he had to follow through on them. In one example, Blackbeard took four hostages from a ship off the coast of South Carolina. The price he demanded for them was medicine to treat the sexually transmitted disease syphilis, which most of his crew had. He threatened

Pirate Parties

One pirate stereotype that appears to have been true is their love of alcohol. While some captains did not allow drinking on their ship, others did. Many cargoes included rum, which was made in the Caribbean in the 1600s and was regularly shipped to Europe to supply drinking needs there. Blackbeard wrote in what some people claim is his personal journal:

1718. Rum all out. Our Company somewhat sober—A ... confusion amongst us! Rogues a plotting [talk of mutiny or desertion] ... so I look'd sharp for a Prize.

(Later) Took one with a great deal of Liquor on Board, so kept the company hot [drunk] ... then all things went well again.[51]

In addition to rum, pirate ships had on board a kind of alcoholic drink known as grog or bumbo. Bumbo

Rum was generally stored in barrels similar to these.

was a mixture of rum, water, sugar, and nutmeg. It was not as strong as straight rum, so pirates could drink it in moderate quantities and still be ready to work when necessary. They may also have drunk sangaree, which is now called sangria—red wine with fruit in it. The most common fruits used to make sangria are citrus fruits such as lemons, limes, and oranges. These fruits would have been helpful in preventing attacks of scurvy, which is a disease people get when there is too little vitamin C in their diet.

Pirates also celebrated by eating any good foods that were found on board the captured ships. Ordinary pirate food included hardtack biscuits (similar to crackers), salmagundi (a stew of whatever the cook had on hand, which could include chopped meat, fish, onions, and spices), salted beef, eggs if there were chickens on board, and pickled vegetables. Therefore, any change of menu was welcome, and after capturing a ship, pirates ate and enjoyed themselves without a thought for good manners or saving anything for another day. George Francis Dow and John Henry Edmonds wrote, "They passed the time away, drinking and carousing merrily, before and after dinner, which they eat in a very disorderly manner, more like a kennel of hounds, than like men, snatching and catching the victuals [food] from one another."[52]

Pirate Treasure

More important than food or drink was the treasure that remained. As in fiction, ships often carried chests of coins. Some of the most well known were Spanish silver dollars, also called pieces of eight because they were the equivalent of eight reals (another Spanish silver coin). Other coins that made up pirate treasure were gold doubloons, equal to 32 reals.

Legend has it that pirates commonly buried chests of coins and treasure and then created maps so they or other pirates could relocate them. No authentic treasure maps have ever been found, however, probably because most pirates quickly spent or sold their treasure.

Despite the lure of treasure, by the 1730s, the chances of pirates being able to steal a fortune were slim. Their attacks had affected too many countries, and tolerance for them was wearing thin. European nations were building up their navies in order to offer greater protection for merchants and to hunt down the outlaws. Earle wrote, "And so at last the golden age of piracy came to an end. The freedom and drink-loving pirates had their moment of fame, but in the long run the navy, the law and the self-destructive nature of the pirates themselves ensured that piracy was not an occupation with a very long life expectancy."[53]

Such was not the case in Asia, however. Though less famous than their European counterparts, Asian pirates pillaged ships and villages long after the Golden Age of Piracy faded. Under their influence, piracy flourished in the South China Sea and pirate empires were built that lasted hundreds of years.

CHAPTER FOUR

ASIAN PIRATES

Asia was not exempt from the piracy that took place everywhere else in the ancient world. Konstam wrote,

In Chinese waters the threat of piracy remained constant for seafarers for more than a thousand years, probably longer. The first recorded incident ... in the South China Sea took place in a.d. 589 ... However, it is almost a certainty that piracy flourished long before.[54]

Like the Barbary pirates, Asian pirates' lives and customs were not as well documented as those who sailed during the Golden Age, and conflicting accounts can often be found.

Asian Pirates' Territory

The South China Sea is the part of the Pacific Ocean that lies south of mainland China, west of the Philippines, and north of Indonesia. As in other parts of the world, piracy existed there because people living along the coasts were skilled at navigation and were desperate enough to steal to make a living. Like the Barbary and Caribbean pirates, no governments or navies could stop them because these men were familiar with the area and could hide from their pursuers. Even when the powerful Ming dynasty arose in China, it was unable to abolish the practice. In fact, money spent by governments to suppress piracy was often channeled through corrupt officials to pirates who used it to increase their own power.

In making their attacks, Asian pirates relied on a traditional boat called a junk. The name comes from the Malay word *jong*, which means "ship." The junk was a wide, flat-bottomed vessel, invented as early as the second century. It was commonly used as a merchant ship or warship. Junks had up to four masts with triangular

Many Asian pirates sailed a ship called a junk (shown here).

bamboo sails, and their holds were divided into small compartments so the entire ship would not flood if one part was damaged. Some of the largest junks measured over 100 feet (30.5 m) and had more than 200 people in a crew. The average, however, was around 45 feet (14 m) with just a few dozen crew members.

Pirates converted merchant junks to pirate ships by adding 10 to 30 large guns, including at least one *lantaka*, or swivel cannon, which they could use to clear enemy decks of any opposition. Between attacks, crews generally slept on deck or in the hold. Historian H. Warington Smyth said, "As an engine for carrying man and his commerce upon the high and stormy seas as well as on the vast inland waterways, it is doubtful if any class of vessel … is more suited or better adapted to its purpose than the Chinese or Indian junk."[55]

Pirate Groups

Sailing in their junks, some of the earliest Asian pirates were Indonesian and Malaysian. As early as the 1400s, for instance, the Orang Laut pirates of Malaysia attacked ships in the Strait of Malacca, while pirates from Borneo (governed by the countries of Brunei, Indonesia, and Malaysia) struck ships in the waters between Singapore and Hong Kong. The Buginese pirates, or Bugis, of Indonesia were said to have targeted Dutch and British East Indies trading ships in the 1600s and 1700s and were known for their ruthlessness and for taking their victims unawares. Camouflaging their ships and themselves in black, they attacked merchant ships in the dark of night, creating great fear. Some believe that when word of them made its way back to Europe, their actions formed the basis for boogeyman stories that frightened children for generations.

Although the Bugis pirates are well known in Asia even today, modern historians have criticized the spread of these stories. According to historian Khoo Kay Kim, the Bugis were not pirates at all; British officials who were living in Malaya made up this story so the British government would extend their authority:

"They needed a reason to give to the British government," Khoo said. "By saying the Malay rulers were pirates, it was easier for them to intervene. The British government would have stopped it if it knew that all this talk of pirates was based on lies." He said there was no way the

Some of the earliest Asian pirates came from Malaysia. Someone who lives in Malaysia is called Malaysian, but members of the native ethnic group are called Malays.

Bugis could be considered pirates because piracy, as defined by the law of the time, could be committed only in areas that had no government.

"The areas around the Straits of Melaka and the South China Sea were all part of the Malay realm of governance and if a ship were to enter the region and not pay toll, then the ruler had the right to attack the ship. That's not piracy."[56]

The wokou were other well-known pirates who sailed out of Japan beginning in the 12th century. Early wokou came from the ranks of Japanese farmers and fishermen, but in later centuries, Chinese, Korean, and other ethnicities joined them as well. According to *Encyclopedia Britannica*, "They were often in the pay of various Japanese feudal leaders and were frequently involved in Japan's civil wars during the early part of this period."[57] No one knows their exact numbers, but at times they ran as few as 20 junks and at other times up to 400. Not only did they attack ships and steal the goods on board, but they also plundered coastlines and extorted tribute from Chinese leaders eager to keep them away from their cities.

One of the worst periods of wokou piracy was the decade between 1376 and 1385, when 174 instances of pirate raids were recorded against Korea alone. Some of these raids involved bands of as many as 3,000 pirates, who looted grain and took captives to be used as slaves or to be held for ransom. Another active wokou period was in the 1500s. Between 1523 and 1588, the wokou made 66 raids on Zhejiang Province on the coast of China, an average of one attack a year. During this period, Chinese pirate chief Wang Zhi was one of the best known of the wokou. He headed a large, well-armed fleet that attacked official establishments such as county and district treasuries, as well as pillaged the general countryside. Because of him and other wokou, townspeople and villagers along the coast built tall fences around their settlements for added security.

In addition to sponsoring piracy, the Japanese were also victims of it. The samurai caste, a respected social group consisting of trained warriors, was originally created in the 9th century to protect wealthy landowners from attacks, including pirate attacks. The samurai were successful in getting foreign pirates to stop their raids, but there were also Japanese pirates who attacked their own country. They were called *kaizoku*, which means "sea robbers." One of these was Fujiwara Sumitomo, an aristocrat who commanded a *kaizoku* fleet. Like William Kidd, he was originally employed by the government to catch pirates but ended up becoming one himself. According to Lewis, "He mounted plundering raids in style and in strength

gave themselves up. However, due to disease and famine, most could not make a permanent living at farming and turned back to piracy. This illustrates an important fact about pirates: Most chose the lifestyle out of desperation when there was no other way to make a living and their government did not have good welfare programs in place. As Lewis wrote, "The land barely yielded a living for many farmers or the sea for many fishermen … For many Japanese, piracy was the only way out."[59] Creating the wokou redirected these pirates toward other countries.

Kanhoji Angre

By the mid-16th century, the wokou had almost entirely disappeared. This was due in part to new trade policies between China and other countries. Because of these policies, more European and American ships came to the East, and the naval power that arrived to protect those ships was an added force in fighting and capturing pirates.

Pirate activity soon arose in other parts of Asia, however. Notable action

One of the duties of early samurai was to fight pirates.

with a fleet numbering around 1000 vessels."[58]

Japan tried to deal with its pirate problem by offering pardons along with a farming "starter kit" of clothes, food, seeds, and land to those who

took place off the west coast of India, where privateer and warrior Kanhoji Angre led a fleet of ships during the 18th century. He and his men operated out of great rowing vessels called *gurabs*, nicknamed "grabs" by the Europeans. These had up to three sails and could carry numerous cannons. According to some, when the sails were spread, the *gurabs* looked like massive cities at sea. The pirates also used smaller galivats, which had only two masts and were more easily navigated close to the coastline.

Angre was a member of the Maratha (warrior) class in India, which was similar to the Japanese samurai, and was the first notable chief of the Maratha navy. In 1698, he was also given control of the western coast of India from Bombay (now Mumbai) to Vingoria (now Vengurla). That stretch of land included 26 forts that had been built for defense purposes. Angre made one of them—Vijaydurg—his primary stronghold. The literal meaning of Vijaydurg is "Victory Fort," and it was located on a small island close to shore. It had been built about AD 1200 and included several unique architectural features: There was a shipbuilding facility, an undersea wall that was invisible to attacking ships, and a triple ring of fortifications. An undersea and underground tunnel also ran from the fort to an estate in the nearby village of Girye.

Angre spent most of his privateer career making bold attacks against large British, Dutch, and Portuguese trading ships that carried goods from India to the West. Those ships belonged to countries that had colonized India, and many Indians resented the occupation of their country by outsiders. Because of his reputation for success against such strong opponents, men from all over the world were willing to work for Angre. These included Indian sailors as well as European mercenaries who were loyal to whoever paid them well. Angre's own ship was manned by a crew of Dutch sailors, and his chief gunner was a former Jamaican pirate.

With men, ships, and strongholds, Angre built a reputation for being invincible. He extorted tribute from Indian and British shipping companies. In 1712, he seized the armed yacht of the East India Company's governor and held it for a large ransom. In 1721, he repelled a British attack on Fort Vijaydurg using specially built gunships. By 1722, Angre's repeated success against the British East India Company led it to abandon any attempts to defeat him. He was considered a pirate by the British, although in reality, he was a government-sponsored privateer just like Sir Francis Drake.

Angre died on June 4, 1729, never having been defeated in battle. It was said by an unidentified source that "had he been in England, like Drake, he would have been knighted and lionised as a national hero, but in India

Like samurai, Maratha warriors protected their country.

he died merely as an independent ruler who never permitted any foreign ruler to filch [take] even a part of his precious little dominion."[60] Recognition finally came in 1951, when the Western Naval Command of the Indian Navy was named INS (Indian Naval Ship) Angre in his honor. A statue of Angre also stands in the Naval Dockyard in Mumbai.

Long-Term Piracy

While pirates such as Angre sailed the seas for relatively short spans of time, Chinese pirates were a long-term problem for Asia. Due to weak governments and the support of regional warlords who dominated sections of the coastline, some pirates were able to form powerful empires that allowed them to pillage and plunder with little fear of consequences. Their attacks were sometimes aimed at those they disagreed with politically, but unlike privateers from other countries, few

Chinese pirates had the backing of a government sponsor while they were sailing the seas.

The first of the three most powerful Chinese pirate empires arose in the 1600s. It was headed by a former businessman named Zheng Zhilong from the Fujian Province, opposite the island of Taiwan. Zheng and his fleet of more than 800 junks sailed up and down the coast, attacking shipping in the mouth of the Yangtze River and as far south as Vietnam. They also demanded and received protection money from ship owners in order to allow them to stay in business.

Zheng caused so much disruption that the head of the Ming dynasty named him admiral of coastal waters and gave him control of the province of Fukien in the hopes that he would give up his lawless ways. Zheng sailed under the Ming dynasty until 1646. At that time, he changed loyalties and allowed a competing dynasty, the Manchus, to capture the province. He continued to rule under the Manchus until the anti-Manchu activities of his son, Zheng Chenggong, became too much for authorities to overlook. Held accountable for his son's activities, Zheng was executed in 1661.

Taking His Father's Place

The second pirate empire began immediately after Zheng Zhilong's death, when Zheng Chenggong, also called Koxinga, assumed his father's position as a pirate leader. A strong supporter of the Ming dynasty, Koxinga concentrated his attacks on Manchu ships, which he plundered and sank. He also used his pirate fleet to lead raids against Manchu-held cities, becoming so successful that the emperor had to order the inhabitants of 80 sea towns to move inland to avoid his attacks.

Koxinga's pirate empire survived into the 1680s despite heavy losses sustained in a failed attempt to drive the Manchu forces from Nanking in 1659. He maintained a tight hold on regional trade for almost 25 years, took on Dutch traders who operated in his region, and captured the island of Formosa (now Taiwan) from the Dutch in 1662.

In 1662, Koxinga died at the age of 37. Although he had been an outlaw all his life, he is remembered in China as a hero. Konstam wrote, "Today … (Koxinga) is seen as a hero, both in Taiwan and in mainland China, where his reputation as a defender of Ming culture and civilization seems to have outweighed his crimes as a pirate warlord."[61]

Creating a New Empire

The third Chinese pirate empire was the most powerful of the three. Famine in 1799 drove many Chinese farmers to become pirates, with entire families of men, women, and children roaming the seas looking for merchant ships to attack. A man named Zheng Yi took advantage of this source of manpower when he began building a coalition of small pirate fleets beginning in 1801.

Zheng Yi was the son of a pirate and was experienced in the trade. In 1801, he married the woman who would later take the name Zheng Yi Sao ("Zheng's widow"), and they put together an alliance of pirates that regularly attacked ships around the Canton area. By 1805, Zheng Yi commanded so many ships that he divided them into six fleets, each known by a color—black, red, white, blue, yellow, and green. Each fleet was assigned an area in which to operate.

Zheng Yi remained with the Red Fleet but retained control over the others to ensure that they did not fight or interfere with each other's operations. The fleets also stood by to help each other if necessary.

When Zheng Yi died in 1807, his wife took over the empire and made it even stronger than it had been when he was alive. After she retired from piracy herself, she opened a gambling house in China. She died in 1844 at the age of 69.

Zheng Yi Sao (pictured here) was one of the most powerful women in history as the commander of a pirate empire.

Joining Forces

Piracy continued in Asia through the 1800s, although the ethnicity of the pirates changed. In the 1830s, 1840s, and 1850s, Asian pirates were joined by British, American, and French renegades who prowled the South China Sea. The latter three came to the region as a result of foreign trade. American pirate Eli Boggs was an example of one of the outsiders. He had a fleet of 30 or more junks and conducted raids on English clipper ships. Boggs was known for being handsome and charming, as *London Times* correspondent

HUNTING PIRATES

Many people tried to make a living by hunting and capturing pirates. These people were often employed by a government. One of the first recorded pirate hunters was Pompey, a friend of Julius Caesar's as well as a military and political leader in Rome in the first century BC. The problem of piracy was so great in the Mediterranean that he was given almost the entire contents of the Roman treasury to build a fleet of 500 ships and raise an army of 120,000 men. With this fleet, Pompey effectively removed all piracy from the area in less than a year.

Most pirate hunters became famous only if they captured a lot of pirates or if their targets included notorious pirates. In 1718, for instance, colonial leader William Rhett led a naval expedition against Stede Bonnet, the Gentleman Pirate, and captured him off Cape Fear, North Carolina. That same year, Robert Maynard became a household name when he killed Blackbeard off the coast of North Carolina. Woodes Rogers, English sea captain, privateer, and the first royal governor of the Bahamas, was perhaps the most renowned pirate hunter. Rogers accepted the task of bringing law to the Bahamas in 1718 and began by offering pardons to those pirates who wanted to turn themselves in. At the same time, he captured and made examples of those who chose to fight. His efforts led to the public hanging of eight pirates. In Asia, although many people tried to capture Zheng Yi Sao, she always escaped; eventually the government had no choice but to offer her a pardon.

George Wingrove Cook testified in 1857: "It was a face of feminine beauty … Large lustrous eyes; a mouth the smile of which might woo a coy maiden; affluent black hair, not carelessly parted … such was the Hong Kong pirate Eli Boggs."[62]

Although handsome, Boggs was also cruel. In one case, he had the body of a captured Chinese merchant cut into small pieces and delivered to shore in small buckets as a warning against interference in his criminal activities. He was eventually captured and imprisoned for piracy, but it is reported that the jury did not charge him with murder because they could not believe someone so young and good-looking could be so ruthless. Since none of his fellow pirates would testify against him, he was sentenced to only three years in a Hong Kong prison.

The 20th century saw continued pirate activity in Asia. Between 1921 and 1929, there were 29 major pirate attacks on river steamers, cargo ships, and other vessels off the coast of southern China. Fifty-one major attacks were recorded off the Asian coast between World War I and World War II. In December 1947, the Dutch ship *Van Heutsz* was captured by Asian pirates, who robbed the passengers of more than $90,000.

Even up to the present day, the oceans around Asia have been the site of piracy, hijacking, and murder. However, the problem is not confined to Asia; other parts of the world are plagued by modern piracy, too. Whether in the South China Sea or off the coast of Somalia, authorities have found that today's pirates are just as ruthless as their predecessors and just as hard to control. Maritime expert Nur Jale wrote in 2009, "After a long absence, the world's seas have once again become the pirate's playground. Piracy is on the rise … and is becoming increasingly complex, better organized, and more violent."[63]

PIRATES AT SEA AND ON LAND

Although pirates no longer captain galleys and dress in colorful outfits, they still exist. As with most historical pirates, many modern pirates can be found in the waters around poorer coastal countries with few economic options. For these men and women, the transition from sailor to pirate is often an easy one. They are willing to risk danger to support themselves and their families.

Less dangerous but more common are internet pirates. These can be found all over the world, thanks to the increasing ease of downloading content. There are many reasons why people illegally download movies, music, software, and other things that can be widely found online. This has become one of the 21st century's most common crimes. Although internet pirates do not often face bodily injury the way maritime pirates do, illegal downloading does carry its own risks.

A Heavily Targeted Area

The Strait of Malacca is a 550-mile (885 km) stretch of water between the Malaysian Peninsula and the Indonesian island of Sumatra. It is extremely narrow, only 1.7 miles (2.7 km) across at its smallest point. In the 1800s, the strait was an important passageway for commercial ships traveling between China and India. In modern times, it is part of the route between the busy ports of eastern Asia and ports in Europe and the Middle East. Nearly 100,000 ships pass through the strait annually, making it one of the world's busiest trading routes.

The strait is a challenge for ship owners and mariners because their ships must slow down to navigate its length. Once slowed down, the ships are easy for pirates to attack. The strait is also dotted with thousands of small islands, ideal locations for pirates to hide and avoid capture. In 2000, there were 75 pirate attacks in the Strait of Malacca,

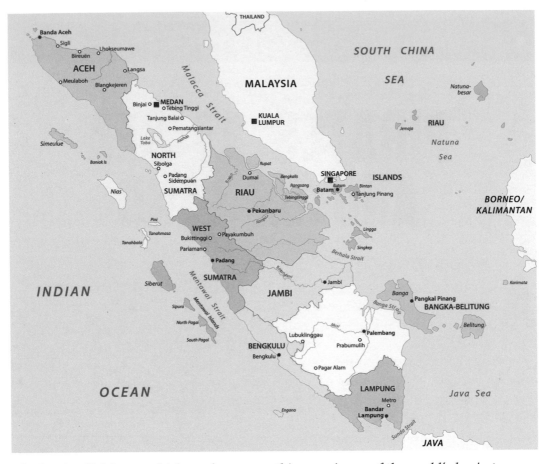

The Strait of Malacca, which can be seen on this map, is one of the world's busiest shipping routes, making it a prime target for pirates.

28 in 2003, 38 in 2004, and 79 in 2005; in total, between 1995 and 2013, 41 percent of the world's pirate attacks took place in Southeast Asia, where the strait is located. So great was the continuing risk that, in 2005, the renowned insurance company Lloyds of London began charging more to insure anything that would pass through the area, and in 2014, the United Nations (UN) named it the most dangerous waterway in the world.

In addition to the physical aspects of the strait that encourage piracy, pirates have taken advantage of the fact that the waterway is not under the control of a single country. Indonesia controls the majority of the sea-lane, but Malaysia and Singapore, an independent city-state, control the rest. All of these areas have different maritime security policies. Different agencies are responsible for different aspects of piracy in Malaysia, making for bureaucratic

DEFINING MODERN PIRACY

The following acts are included in the modern definition of piracy:

- boarding
- extortion
- hostage taking
- kidnapping of people for ransom
- murder
- robbery
- sabotage resulting in the ship subsequently sinking
- seizure of items or the ship
- shipwrecking

complications and slowdowns. Indonesia and other cash-strapped governments have not been able to afford adequate coast guard and naval forces, so patrol of their territories is incomplete. These inconsistencies mean that pirates can move from one country's jurisdiction to another and evade pursuit and capture.

Who Are the Pirates?

The majority of modern pirates who prowl the waters around Asia are of Indonesian origin. Most are native seafaring people who live in coastal villages along the strait. Like historical pirates, most are poor, and some are outlaws who have turned to piracy as a means of easy profit. In their book *Jolly Roger with an Uzi*, lawyers Jack A. Gottschalk and Brian P. Flanagan wrote, "There seems to be one primary cause for the sharp rise in pirate activity, namely the general downturn in the international economy."[64] They steal cash and electronics that can be found on board ships that they hijack. Many of these are their victims' personal possessions, and sometimes they have sentimental as well as financial value, which makes their theft even more upsetting. Some earn wages by working for corrupt customs or coast guard officials who profit from piracy. Others are part of organized crime syndicates.

According to Gottschalk and Flanagan, the main threat from pirates is not theft, it is injury. The amount pirates steal is often not enough to bother a major company; however, they not only rob crews but also kidnap seamen for ransom—a practice that poses less danger for the pirates than stealing items,

Cash and electronics are two of the things that are most commonly stolen by modern pirates.

according to the organization Oceans Beyond Piracy—and sailors often face the threat of murder.

According to Captain Pottengal Mukundan, director of the International Maritime Bureau (IMB), "There's nothing romantic about piracy. These are ruthless people who are heavily armed and prey on people that are weaker than them."[65]

Somali Pirates

While the Strait of Malacca has been one of the most pirate-plagued regions of the modern world, piracy off the Somali coast is better known by Americans. Somalia is a country on the northeast coast of Africa. It is bordered by Kenya to the south, the Gulf of Aden to the north, the Indian Ocean to the east, and Ethiopia to the west. The region is part of the Horn of Africa, a 772,200-square-mile

(2 million sq km) peninsula that juts out into the Arabian Sea.

From 1991 to the present, Somalia has endured civil war and the lack of a strong central government. The country's provisional government does not control the semi-independent regional governments of Somaliland and Puntland, both in northeastern Somalia. Security forces are weak, and corruption is widespread. Tribal or clan struggles add to the disruption, and criminal networks are able to operate freely.

Foreign companies who took advantage of the disruption in Somalia in the 1990s also created justification for piracy in the minds of some Somalis. The native fishing industry was hard-hit after commercial fishing companies from Europe, Arabia, and eastern Asia began illegally fishing off the Somali coast and illegally dumping industrial waste in offshore areas. With no effective coast guard to protect their shores, locals felt justified attacking the intruders. Maritime risk consultant Michael G. Frodl wrote, "When [fighting off foreign fishermen] proved ineffective, some realized that 'fishing' for foreign ships [piracy] was more rewarding than going after dwindling fish stocks."[66]

Between 2005 and 2012, Somali pirates were a significant threat. In 2012, increased naval patrols in the area, as well as improvements in the stability of the Somali government, essentially stopped the threat of Somali piracy. However, in 2017, the pirates began hijacking ships again, leading to fears of a renewed threat. According to the British newspaper *Telegraph*, the pirates may have become active again because "anti-piracy patrols run by Western navies have been drastically reduced in the past year so that ships can be reassigned to cope with the migrant crisis in the Mediterranean and threats from Russia in the Baltic."[67]

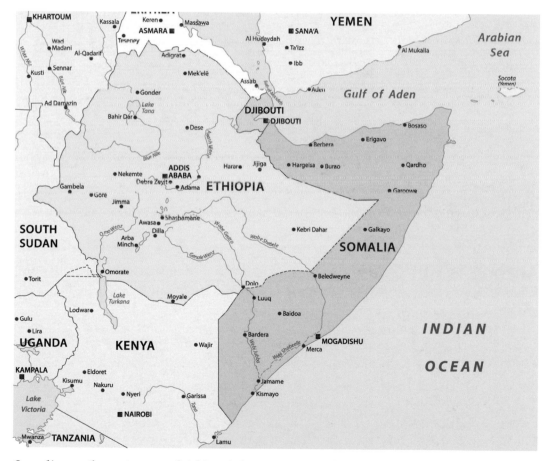

Somalia, on the east coast of Africa, is home to some of the most infamous modern pirates.

MODERN PIRATES IN THE MEDIA

Although historical pirates are seen in popular culture as fun and cool, modern pirates are portrayed much more realistically but far less frequently. One movie that dealt with this topic was the 2013 film *Captain Phillips*, starring Tom Hanks. It is based on the story of the 2009 hijacking of the *Maersk Alabama*. In the movie, Phillips, played by Hanks, must negotiate with the pirates to save his crew. Although the movie received good reviews, it was criticized by the real crew of the *Maersk Alabama*, who said the event did not happen anything like the way it is shown in the movie. According to them, Phillips ignored warnings of pirates as they sailed near the Somali coast, deliberately putting them all in danger.

Captain Phillips is one of the few movies that deals with modern-day piracy.

Anyone Is Fair Game

When it comes to choosing their victims, the Somali pirates are not particular about whom they attack. Commercial ships are favored because they are slower and their cargo is worth millions of dollars, but even cruise ships and privately owned tourist vessels can be hit. Author and sailing enthusiast Jamie Furlong wrote, "Pirates are after the big ships, but if they are unsuccessful they'll begin to run out of supplies and will therefore have no hesitation in taking on a sail boat or fishing boat in order to replenish their stocks of food and water."[68]

Attacks can come at any time of the day and are generally made in multiple small motorboats. These boats generally set out from a "mother ship," where the pirates live between attacks. A mother ship is a larger vessel, sometimes a

Most modern pirate attacks are carried out in small, fast boats.

that the pirates were getting ready to start up again.

When making an attack, the pirates approach rapidly from multiple directions. They generally carry automatic weapons such as AK-47s and reloadable, shoulder-fired grenade launchers such as the RPG-7 to intimidate the unarmed ship's crew into slowing down to allow boarding. In the confusion that is created, long, lightweight ladders are used to climb aboard so pirates can take control of the vessel and steer it into a pirate-friendly port.

Ignoring the Risks

Although pirate attacks can be deadly for the victims, they are not the only ones who face danger. A Somali pirate's career is a perilous one. There is the risk of retaliation from ships' crews or navy vessels that respond to calls for help. Pirates also deal with bad weather and accidents. Every week, men and equipment are lost at sea. For instance, the drowned body of one of the men who helped seize a ship called the *Sirius Star* in 2009 later washed ashore with his share of the ransom still on his body. Nevertheless, the pirates continue to attack because to them, the financial gains outweigh the risks.

Like pirates of old, modern pirates are looking for treasure, and Somali pirates have discovered that big money can be made by holding commercial ships and their crews for ransom.

pirated merchant ship, that is used as a floating base of operations. It can hold large stores of weapons and supplies and is more stable in bad weather than the small motorboats pirates use to carry out their attacks. This allows pirates to go farther from shore and attack at any time of the year. In 2011, authorities determined that up to eight mother ships were stationed off the coast of Somalia, providing protection for pirates and a place to hold hostages. In May 2017, pirates hijacked a small Iranian fishing boat, which officials say is likely to be used as a mother ship. This indicated

Owners of one Chinese ship that was captured off Somalia in 2009 paid $4 million for its release. The Greek-owned *Maran Centaurus*, carrying $140 million worth of crude oil in 2009, was released in January 2010 after a ransom of between $5.5 million and $7 million was paid. Although the ransoms are large, the amounts are small in comparison to the value of the ships and the cargoes, so companies are willing to pay rather than risk losing everything. In addition to ships and their crews, private individuals are held for ransom. Families on small yachts are sometimes taken and held on their own ships, on ships that had previously been pirated, or in the case of Paul and Rachel Chandler of England, in isolated bush camps on land. The Chandlers were captured on their 38-foot (11.6 m) sailboat off the Seychelles on October 23, 2009. They were released on November 14, 2010, after a reported $800,000 was paid.

New Hiding Places

While waiting for ransoms to be paid, the pirates often return to towns where they are relatively safe from pursuit, the way historical pirates hid in places such as Tortuga and Port Royal. In the past, Somali ports such as Eyl, Bossaso, and Garad have been pirate havens, but the Puntland government took steps to make arrests there, causing pirates to move elsewhere. One pirate haven that was active in 2011 was a village called Harardhere. That year, religious extremists attacked Harardhere, demanding a portion of the pirates' takings. After this event, many of the outlaws moved north to Hobyo, another pirate stronghold. Ships were anchored offshore there, and 10-year-old boys with automatic weapons patrolled the streets, on the lookout for strangers who might be extremists or authorities. The pirate presence was everywhere in Hobyo, and even villagers who were not involved in piracy appreciated how it helped the town; for instance, the pirates set up a form of social security for those in need. The town's car dealer, who made his living selling expensive cars to pirates after they received a large ransom, pointed out, "They have allocated $100,000 to help those who are outside their business and not working."[69] This shows that like their historical counterparts, modern pirates have some progressive ideals. However, some residents criticized the fact that most of the pirates' money was spent on themselves rather than improving the town.

Splitting the Loot

When ransoms were agreed upon, they were often paid in dollars or euros and delivered in sturdy sacks or waterproof cases. Delivery could be by helicopter drop, by boat, or even by parachute, an event that happened in January 2009, when $3 million in cash was paid to pirates that hijacked the *Sirius Star*.

Once the ransom was paid, the pirates used sophisticated currency-counting machines to tally totals and check for

Some residents of the village of Hobyo benefited from the pirates' presence, but others did not.

counterfeit bills. Then they divided up the money. "Generally, roughly 30 percent of the ransom goes to the investors, 20 percent goes to the government officials and port officials or even Islamists who guard the boat while negotiations are going on,"[70] said J. Peter Pham, an expert on Somali pirate financing at James Madison University in Harrisburg, Virginia. The remaining 50 percent went to the pirates themselves, with those who actually boarded the ship getting a cut that ranged from $10,000 to $20,000. At that time in Somalia, the average income was $500 annually, so the payoff was worth the risk. The money was often used to buy new cell phones and cars, build large houses, and pay for extravagant lifestyles.

Dividing the spoils was just as dangerous as any other part of the operation, however. The crew would be joined by shopkeepers from the shore who had been taking care of the hostages and wanted to be paid. Arguments and fights would often break out. Hostages were often caught in the middle of a chaotic situation. Captain Andrey Nozhkin of a Danish-owned merchant ship called the *CEC Future* was captured by pirates in November 2008. He recalled the day the ship's

The civil war in Somalia is one reason why it is hard for most Somalis to earn a good living, which is why many people are willing to risk becoming pirates.

ransom was paid in January 2009. "Those accused of trying to take too much had their hands slammed in doors as a punishment. Then some of the pirates started shooting, some were fighting with knives. Then other boats started arriving trying to get on board and people on the boat began shooting at them."[71]

Despite such disorganization, pirates have proven difficult to completely get rid of in the 21st century. Technology and improved communication systems should make catching them easier, but there are still challenges to their capture and prosecution. Vice Admiral Mike Fox, commander of U.S. Naval Forces Central Command in the Middle East, said,

The piracy issue requires a mosaic of different people working together— from creating the rule of law ashore in Somalia, industry leaders using best management practices, the military to patrol, disrupt and deter the pirates, and finally we need an appropriate legal "finish," so that when we catch people in the act, they're able to be taken to justice. It's an international problem and it's going to take an international cooperative solution.[72]

Fighting Maritime Piracy

When piracy again became a significant risk for ships in the 1980s, some countries had not thought of the problem for decades. Some discovered they did not even have established piracy laws. As pirate activity swelled and began to affect international shipping lanes, action and cooperation between governments lagged. To make matters worse, shipping companies hesitated to report pirate attacks because it was time-consuming, led to delays that cost thousands of dollars a day, and caused insurance costs to rise.

Those who wanted to do something faced confusion over how piracy was legally defined. There was no consistency worldwide, and that sometimes provided loopholes for pirates to escape capture and punishment. For instance, the IMB, a nonprofit organization formed in 1981 to fight all kinds of maritime crime, defined piracy as "an act of boarding (or attempted boarding) with the intent to commit theft or any other crime and with the intent or capability to use force in furtherance of that act."[73]

On the other hand, the United Nations Convention on the Law of the Sea (UNCLOS) of 1982 stated that maritime piracy was any act of violence committed for private reasons by the crew of one ship against another on the high seas. The term "high seas" was significant because that meant that, according to the United Nations, pirate attacks within territorial waters—within 12 miles (19.3 km) of a country's coastline—were not classified as piracy. Thus, in some cases, pirates who operated within or escaped into a country's territorial waters (as is the case in the Strait of Malacca) could not be pursued by officials from another country. If the pirates fled into the waters of a country such as Somalia, which did not have the will or the means to go after its own pirates within its own territorial waters, they were able to escape. According to Gottschalk and Flanagan, creating anti-piracy laws has been difficult because it requires mixing national and international law, as well as an understanding that "legal" is a broad term:

> If an act of piracy occurs within the territorial jurisdiction of the [closest country], the act may be punishable by laws that do not use the word "piracy." Those criminal laws may include such terms as larceny, robbery, murder, kidnapping, battery, and the like ... Only acts that do not occur within the territorial jurisdiction of a nation are truly termed piracy.[74]

In other words, while people are clearly committing criminal acts, they cannot be charged with piracy unless their crimes occurred in international waters, which do not belong to any particular country.

Protecting Themselves

Without strong protection from authorities, those who sailed through pirate-infested waters in the early

21st century were on their own when it came to defending themselves. A group of international shipping and trading organizations, as well as the European Union (EU), North Atlantic Treaty Organization (NATO), and the IMB, soon published a handbook that became the authoritative guide for those who needed to protect themselves. The handbook is now in its fourth printing and is titled *Best Management Practices to Deter Piracy off the Coast of Somalia and in the Arabian Sea Area* (BMP4). As of 2018, officials are working on a fifth edition.

BMP4 advises that, as a first step, ships should let their crew know they are sailing through pirate-infested waters and make sure the crew is aware of the proper procedure to take in case of attack. These may include posting extra lookouts and giving them kevlar jackets, also called bulletproof vests. They should then proceed through the area as quickly as possible. Crews should be continually on the lookout for pirates, using binoculars and night goggles. They should recognize potential threats, particularly small boats filled with many armed men, and take immediate steps, including calling for naval support. The ship should be fitted with a distinctive pirate alarm, and safe areas should be created where the crew can retreat in the event pirates get on board.

To make it harder for pirates to board, ships' decks should be ringed with coils of razor wire, and fire hoses or other water systems should be installed to spray powerful jets or walls of water over the sides. The water can be seawater, hot water, or even electrically charged water. Spraying slippery foam on decks and over the sides is another option to hinder boarding.

Working Together

Although it took time, by 2009, modern piracy was recognized as a global problem, and different nations began to come together to help curb attacks. For instance, the Combined Task Force 151 (CTF-151) is one of three anti-piracy task forces that are part of the U.S.-led Combined Maritime Forces (CMF), a multinational naval partnership that promotes security, stability, and prosperity in the Middle East. CMF is made up of more than 20 countries, including the United States, Canada, South Korea, France, and the United Kingdom. Members contribute intelligence personnel, surgical teams, and helicopter squadrons, among other things. Vice Admiral Bill Gortney, CMF commander in 2009, noted, "The problem of piracy is and continues to be a problem that begins ashore and is an international problem that requires an international solution. We believe the establishment of CTF-151 is a significant step in the right direction."[75]

Once pirates are caught, prosecuting them can be difficult. Because the Somali government does not have the desire or the means to deal with all cases of piracy, the country involved in

ANTI-PIRATE TECHNOLOGY

While small companies or independent vessels can often afford only basic anti-piracy measures, larger companies have begun using more advanced technology. Some equip their ships with anti-piracy weapons such as sonic devices that send a powerful sound wave out to a directed target, bursting eardrums and causing pirates to become disoriented enough to drop their weapons; a gun that covers boarding pirates with a liquid that smells bad and burns their skin, causing them to jump into the water to wash it off; and a dazzle gun, which is a device that shines a light in pirates' eyes to blind them. Non-lethal attacks are generally preferred. For one thing, they are less dangerous for the sailors to use because they do not risk harming any crewmates who get in the way or prompting revenge attacks from the pirates. For another, most people do not like the idea of killing another human if it can be avoided, even one who is attacking them. However, some people say lethal weapons should be allowed on ships because they would prevent pirates from boarding at all.

capturing the outlaws generally takes responsibility for imprisoning them and bringing them to trial. The captor country also has to take responsibility for the costs of the pirates' imprisonment and trial. With trials scheduled in a variety of places, prosecutors sometimes spend much time and money arranging transportation for witnesses and finding translators for the pirates.

Despite the difficulties, some piracy trials have taken place. For example, in May 2010, a Yemeni court sentenced six Somali pirates to death and jailed six others for ten years each for the 2009 hijacking of a Yemeni oil tanker that left one crew member dead. The first trial by a Western country opened in the Netherlands in May 2010. The five defendants were arrested in the Gulf of Aden in January 2009 while allegedly preparing to board the cargo ship *Samanyolu*, registered in the Dutch Antilles. The pirates were found guilty and sentenced to five years in prison. The United States put its first captured pirates on trial in a federal court in Virginia in November 2010. Five Somalis were found guilty of attacking the USS *Nicholas* while it was on patrol off the Somali coast in April 2010. They were given life sentences. FBI agent Janice K. Fedarcyk stated, "Today's charges should send a clear message to those who attempt to engage in piracy against Americans or American vessels—even on the

Although prosecuting pirates is difficult, it has been done. Shown here are four Somali men who were charged with piracy in 2012.

open ocean, you are not beyond the reach of American justice."[76]

Online Piracy

Digital piracy is quite different than maritime piracy, but it is still a crime. It is similar to historical and modern piracy in that it involves theft in a location that does not belong to anyone in particular. In this analogy, the internet is similar to international waters. People can be prosecuted for theft by their home country, but the internet itself does not belong to anyone.

Internet piracy is a surprisingly complex issue. Some people will say it is absolutely wrong because anything illegal is wrong. Others disagree, claiming that some laws are unfair and should not be enforced. Many people do not even consider their actions to be illegal or are unaware that they can be punished for them. To make the issue more complicated, some instances of downloading (saving files onto a computer) or streaming (receiving the files continuously but not saving them permanently) are legal, and others are illegal. It is important to note that the act of downloading or streaming something is not illegal; the illegal act is downloading or streaming copyright-protected material for free. A copyright is a legal right given to a person or company to be the only one allowed to decide what to do with the thing that is copyrighted. For example, if Marvel Studios copyrights its movies, it can choose to give them away for free or charge money for them, but no one else is allowed to do the same thing.

Why Do People Commit Digital Piracy?

There are several main reasons why people download things illegally. One of the biggest factors is cost. Some people do not want to pay for things at all. If they have the option to download something for free, they will, simply because they can. Others do it because they want something, but they cannot afford the price. This is less common with songs and movies, which generally cost only a few dollars; it is more common with software programs such as Microsoft Word and Adobe Photoshop, which some people need for school or work but cannot afford to buy.

A third factor relating to cost is that people are unwilling to pay for something they plan to use only once. For instance, they may download a movie to watch once with friends. Some people go on to purchase the movie if they like it and want to watch it again; these people consider the illegal download to be a type of free preview and justify their actions by the fact that they later buy it legally. Others simply keep the downloaded movie and watch it whenever they want to. Both actions are examples of internet piracy; purchasing the movie later does not cancel out the illegal action that was taken in the first place.

Another cost-related issue is the fact that some people do not think a particular content creator deserves their money. For instance, some people will pay for things such as artwork, games, or knitting patterns if they are getting them from individuals, but they refuse to pay for things such as music and movies because they do not want to make big companies richer. This is somewhat related to the idea that content costs too much. For instance, someone may download a movie because they think movie theaters charge too much for tickets. However, some people do it for other reasons. For example, if they want to see a movie but do not like an action taken by the studio that made it—such as casting an actor the person does not like—they may download the movie as a way to intentionally cost the studio money. Like the ideal of historical pirates as freedom-loving adventurers, these people generally believe they are fighting back against an organization that is doing something wrong. They may also enjoy the fact that their actions involve some risk, and the thrill of getting away with it may encourage them to keep doing it.

Some reasons for piracy are not related to price at all. One common reason is that even though the world is increasingly connected, not all companies operate in all countries. For

This warning is a familiar sight at the beginning of movies, but many people ignore it.

example, a person who lives in Japan may have a friend who lives in Canada who tells them all about their favorite TV show. If the show is not available in Japan or will not be made available until the following year, the person may download it illegally so they can watch it, too. Additionally, illegal downloading has become so common that it is almost expected. For this reason, people may not even be aware that what they are doing is illegal or may justify their actions by pointing out that nearly everyone does it.

Ethical Arguments

Some people have argued that there is nothing morally wrong with illegal downloading. In their view,

> *intellectual property, in the form of copyright and patents, unfairly restricts access to ideas and expression. They consider illegal downloading to be victimless crime, and do not think it imposes significant cost on anyone. In their view, the serious criminal sanctions that sometimes attach to illegal downloading are draconian [too strict] and unjustified.*[77]

When Napster was first created, it was an illegal file-sharing service that allowed people to download copyrighted music. Today, it operates as a legal streaming service similar to Spotify.

People who hold this view generally believe that it does not matter if a few people download something illegally because the majority of people will choose to pay for it, which makes up the difference. They do not believe it is a problem if a company that already makes millions of dollars loses out on an extra $10.

In the opposite view, people say that "owners of intellectual property deserve just as much protection ... as those who have had their handbags or televisions stolen, including civil and criminal sanction against those who have violated their intellectual property."[78]

In this view, it does not matter whether companies already have millions of dollars. The content they are producing is their property, and they have every right to charge people to use it, especially as that is how they cover the costs of producing future content. Additionally, they point out that if everyone holds the view that their own personal actions will not harm a company, the cumulative, or combined, effect of all these people downloading things will end up causing harm. For example, if 500 people say, "My $10 doesn't matter to this wealthy company," the company will end up losing $5,000, not just $10. Since they are losing money, they may have to increase their prices, which may cause more people to turn to piracy.

How Much of a Problem Is Piracy?

Because it is difficult to find out exact figures on illegal downloading, few studies have been done on this issue. The *Freakonomics* blog noted that while some have claimed piracy "costs the U.S. economy between $200 and $250 billion per year, and is responsible for the loss of 750,000 American jobs,"[79] there is no evidence to support these figures, according to a 2010 report released by the Government Accountability Office. It also noted that in the case of people downloading something because they cannot afford it, those numbers should not be included in the economic cost because they would not have bought the item even if it were not available for free.

One 2012 study performed by economists Brett Danaher of Wellesley College and Joel Waldfogel of the University of Minnesota provided a starting point for examining the data. *Scientific American* explained,

> The researchers compiled a database of the weekend box-office returns for the top 10 movies in 17 different countries over three years. They then split the data into two groups: movies released before [file-sharing website] BitTorrent became popular and those released after.[80]

The study found that when companies release movies in the United States and delay the release of those same movies in other countries, ticket sales decline in other countries because people download the movie rather than waiting for it to come out. This is especially true for science fiction and action movies, which tend to be most popular with people who commit digital piracy.

Additionally, many people do not think about how illegal downloading can hurt emerging artists, such as musicians who are not yet popular. *Forbes* magazine reported,

> *Kimberly James, President of indie label CBM Records, says within two hours of releasing music she has found it illegally downloaded on hundreds of websites. "There actually isn't any less incentive for an up and coming artist's music to be pirated than a famous artist. Pirates scour the web in a 'just in case they make it' scenario to take artists' music and profit illegally, often in countries where we have no legal grounding to sue them."*

> *She says it's a massive battle to get the music down once it's been uploaded, one emerging artists often can't afford. With a very conservative estimate of 10% of music royalties lost to piracy … the loss of royalties on one album sale for someone making $40,000 a year would be the equivalent to Katy Perry losing at least $13.5 million of the $135 million she made last year.*[81]

Because it is difficult to know exactly who is downloading material illegally, how much they are downloading, and how their money is otherwise being spent, it is currently almost impossible to accurately measure all the economic effects of piracy. However, two things are certain: Some individuals and companies are suffering, and digital piracy is illegal.

Weighing the Risks

In addition to harming others, digital pirates take certain risks when they download things illegally. First and foremost, there is the potential for legal trouble. This issue, like the laws regarding modern maritime pirates, is complicated. For instance, before CDs were invented, it was common for people to create mixtapes for themselves by using a cassette player to record songs when they were played on the radio. Cassettes and tape recorders can still be found, although they are increasingly rare, so this is technically still an option—and it is, surprisingly, legal in certain circumstances in the United States. The same is true of using a VCR or DVR system to record things on TV. This is because of a 1984 Supreme Court Case called *Sony Corp. of America v. Universal City Studios*, sometimes nicknamed the "Betamax case" after an early form of videocassette called a Betamax. The Court ruled that if someone records copyrighted material for their own personal use and does not sell it to anyone else, it does not count as copyright infringement—the legal term for digital piracy. However, as

streaming services such as Netflix and Hulu have gotten more popular, they have put language in their terms and conditions forbidding customers from copying the content they present.

Similarly, it is not illegal to lend or give someone copyrighted material. If it were, libraries would not exist, friends would not be able to listen to music with each other, and giving digital media as gifts would be punishable by law. People are legally allowed to buy a CD and then do whatever they want with it—give it away, lend it for a short time, even resell it at a garage sale. This is because of a part of U.S. copyright law called the first sale doctrine, which states that after someone has paid money for an item, the seller no longer has any legal say in what happens to it. However, people who borrow a CD would be committing an illegal act if they rip it to their own computer. This has to do with the fact that they are creating a copy of the material. The money that is paid for the original material covers that particular copy. After that, it does not matter who listens to it as long as they are not keeping a second copy for themselves or to sell to other people.

Copyright law is very complicated; there are all kinds of rules and exceptions that many people never know about. This is why it is risky to do something that could be considered piracy. If someone is caught, the punishment is generally up to five years in jail and a fine of up to $250,000—even if someone was unaware that the act was illegal.

For people who do it repeatedly, the maximum jail time rises to 10 years.

Another risk that comes with digital piracy is the threat of viruses, malware, adware, and other computer issues. Although this is a risk people take whenever they use the internet, the risk increases when someone uses an unsafe website. For instance, if someone uses Google to find results for "free movie downloads," the websites that come up are generally created specifically to target users and place viruses and malware on their computer. These can make computers run slow, steal users' personal information, and cause someone to lose important documents.

Another problem with digital piracy that many people are unaware of is that some criminals make money off of it. While most people who upload content illegally are doing so to share with other people who do not want to pay for it, some organized groups upload content to make large amounts of money. According to the British newspaper the *Independent*,

> So-called "release groups" compete with each other to source content and get it up first, in order to attract the most traffic, downloads and money … With new releases, a "cammer" will be used to record the film at the cinema, and can even upload the content in real-time. Release groups can also use editing software to combine video footage stolen from one source with audio stolen from another.[82]

Once the content is online, the people who run streaming websites can make a large profit from it. The *Independent* noted that officials are unsure whether these are the same people who run release groups or whether the release

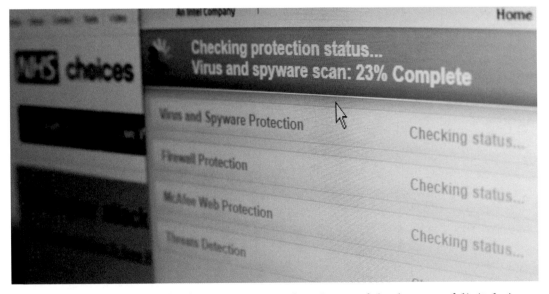

An increased risk of downloading a computer virus is one of the dangers of digital piracy.

groups simply get a portion of the profits for providing the material. They make money through online advertising or by offering paid subscription services to users, but another profitable technique is more harmful:

> [Website] operators "*often steal innocent people's credit card details first, so they can access hundreds of premium channels under those people's names and cover their own tracks. They then put these streams online for their customers to watch and make money from them.*"[83]

These are only a few of the ways people are making money through digital piracy, and it is difficult—if not impossible—for users to know whether the content they are streaming is supporting these large-scale criminals.

Combating Online Piracy

File-sharing networks such as BitTorrent are slightly safer ways of sharing information, and not everything that comes off of them is illegal. Some people put games or other files on BitTorrent because they want people to be able to access it for free. This may be the case if an individual has invented a game or recorded a song but either does not want to or cannot afford to promote it. By making it available for free, many people hope word about their products will spread and people will be more likely to pay money for the next thing they create. However, people also use BitTorrent and other programs like it to share copyrighted material.

This illustrates one reason why the fight against digital piracy is just as complicated as its definition. Making file-sharing websites completely illegal would harm people who use it for legitimate reasons. However, it is difficult to catch people who use it for piracy because the download process is complicated. For instance, if someone is downloading the latest Avengers movie, they are not just getting the movie from one source. They are getting it from multiple computers, called seeds. Each seed gives the target computer one portion of the download, and the target computer pieces them together in the correct order as it receives them. Whenever someone downloads something, their internet protocol (IP) address, which is like a fingerprint that is unique to each computer, can be logged. When companies see that one particular IP address is uploading or downloading a lot of their content, they can ask the internet service provider (ISP) to give them the name of the person the IP address belongs to. Theoretically, this could prove that someone was downloading content illegally. However, in 2014, several federal judges ruled that IP address alone was not enough to charge someone with digital piracy. This is because the IP address only indicates the computer used, not the person who is using it at the time. For instance, if someone uses their mother's computer, the mother

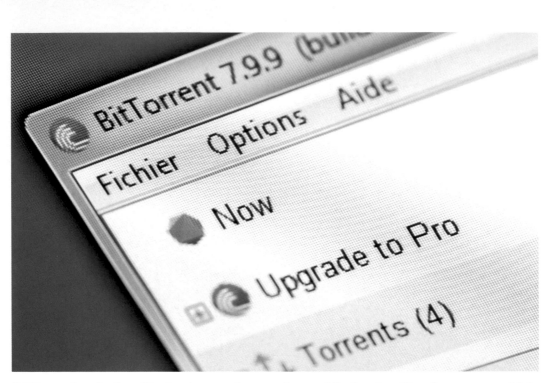

BitTorrent and other file-sharing services can be used for legal or illegal purposes, which means it is not practical to simply make these services illegal.

might be the one charged with piracy even though she did not know about it. Additionally, there are ways for people to hide their IP address and make it look like they are using a different one.

As of 2018, catching and prosecuting illegal downloaders and sharers is difficult and spotty. One person may be made an example of with a high-profile lawsuit while thousands of other, more active digital pirates are either never caught or simply receive letters from their ISP warning them that they know what the person is up to. Some have suggested that the laws should be changed. They have pointed out that stealing a purse is different than stealing copyrighted information, therefore the penalties for both types of theft should not be the same.

More work needs to be done to solve this issue, but this does not mean there is no chance of getting caught and punished. People who do not want to commit a crime or suffer punishment should use alternate methods of getting the media they want. Borrowing things from friends or a library, using legal streaming services such as Netflix and Spotify, or asking for the media they want as holiday and birthday gifts are free or low-cost ways to enjoy media legally.

Notes

Introduction:
Myths Versus Reality

1. Peter Earle, *The Pirate Wars*. New York, NY: Thomas Dunne, 2003, p. 7.

2. Quoted in Earle, *The Pirate Wars*, p. 9.

3. Edward E. Leslie, *Desperate Journeys, Abandoned Souls: True Stories of Castaways and Other Survivors*. New York, NY: Houghton Mifflin, 1988, p. 87.

4. Angus Konstam, *Piracy: The Complete History*. New York, NY: Osprey, 2008, p. 303.

Chapter One:
Piracy in the Mediterranean

5. The Editors of *Encyclopedia Britannica*, "Barbary Pirate," *Encyclopedia Britannica*, accessed November 11, 2017. www.britannica.com/topic/Barbary-pirate.

6. Cindy Vallar, "When Is a Pirate Not a Pirate?," *Pirates and Privateers: The History of Maritime Piracy*, accessed November 29, 2017. www.cindyvallar.com/definitions.html.

7. Earle, *The Pirate Wars*, p. 49.

8. Quoted in Konstam, *Piracy*, p. 91.

9. Stanley Lane-Poole and James Douglas Jerrold Kelley, *The Story of the Barbary Corsairs*. New York, NY: Putnam, 1890, p. 52.

10. Konstam, *Piracy*, p. 83.

11. Lane-Poole and Kelley, *The Story of the Barbary Corsairs*, p. 229.

12. Quoted in Leslie Hotson, "Pirates in Parchment," *The Atlantic*, August 1927. www.theatlantic.com/past/docs/issues/27aug/hotson.htm.

13. "Thomas Jefferson, First Annual Message to Congress," Avalon Project, Yale Law School, December 8, 1801. avalon.law.yale.edu/19th_century/jeffmes1.asp.

14. Konstam, *Piracy*, p. 94.

15. Earle, *The Pirate Wars*, p. 90.

Chapter Two:
The Real Pirates of the Caribbean

16. Rene Chartrand, *The Spanish Main, 1492–1800*. New York, NY: Osprey, 2006, p. 18.

17. The Editors of *Encyclopedia Britannica*, "Spanish Main," *Encyclopedia Britannica*, accessed November 25, 2017. www.britannica.com/place/Spanish-Main.

18. Quoted in Konstam, *Piracy*, p. 61.

19. Philip Gosse, *The History of Piracy*. New York, NY: Longmans, Green and Co., 1932, p. 142.

20. Quoted in Captain Charles Johnson, *A General History of the Pyrates*. London, UK: Warner, 1724, pp. 272–273.

21. Gosse, *The History of Piracy*, p. 145.

22. Earle, *The Pirate Wars*, p. 94.

23. Konstam, *Piracy*, p. 115.

24. Quoted in Stephen Talty, *Empire of the Blue Water*. New York, NY: Crown, 2007, pp. 139–140.

25. Quoted in Larry Gragg, "The Port Royal Earthquake," *History Today*, September 2000, p. 30.

26. Nick Davis, "Jamaica's 'Wickedest City' Port Royal Banks on Heritage," BBC News, July 25, 2012. www.bbc.com/news/world-latin-america-18601357.

27. The Editors of *Encyclopedia Britannica*, "Sir Henry Morgan," *Encyclopedia Britannica*, accessed November 26, 2017. www.britannica.com/biography/Henry-Morgan-Welsh-buccaneer.

28. The Editors of *Encyclopedia Britannica*, "Sir Henry Morgan."

29. Konstam, *Piracy*, p. 251.

Chapter Three:
Pirate Culture

30. David Cordingly, *Under the Black Flag: The Romance and the Reality of Life Among the Pirates*. New York, NY: Random House, 1995, p. xx.

31. Devin Leigh, "Review of *A General History of the Pyrates* by Captain Charles Johnson," *Zamani Reader*, February 23, 2015.

thezamanireader.com/2015/02/23/review-of-a-general-history-of-the-pyrates-by-captain-charles-johnson.

32. Earle, *The Pirate Wars*, p. 101.

33. Vallar, "Oh to Be a Pirate," *Pirates and Privateers*, accessed November 29, 2017. www.cindyvallar.com/bepirate.html.

34. Brenda Ralph Lewis, *The History of Pirates*. London, UK: Amber Books Ltd, 2017, p. 77.

35. Quoted in Johnson, *A General History of the Pyrates*, p. 232.

36. Quoted in Earle, *The Pirate Wars*, p. 172.

37. Amy Crawford, "The Gentleman Pirate," *Smithsonian*, July 31, 2007. www.smithsonianmag.com/history/the-gentleman-pirate-159418520.

38. Quoted in Johnson, *A General History of the Pyrates*, p. 77.

39. Quoted in Konstam, *Piracy*, p. 185.

40. Johnson, *A General History of the Pyrates*, p. 161.

41. Quoted in Konstam, *Piracy*, p. 185.

42. Quoted in Kristy Puchko, "9 Female Pirates You Should Know About," Mental Floss, September 19, 2014. mentalfloss.com/article/58889/9-female-pirates-you-should-know.

43. Puchko, "9 Female Pirates You Should Know About."

44. Earle, *The Pirate Wars*, p. 105.

45. Quoted in Cordingly, *Under the Black Flag*, p. 10.

46. Quoted in Cordingly, *Under the Black Flag*, p. 117.

47. Quoted in Konstam, *Piracy*, p. 118.

48. Quoted in Konstam, *Piracy*, p. 216.

49. Johnson, *A General History of the Pyrates*, p. 390.

50. Johnson, *A General History of the Pyrates*, pp. 87–88.

51. Gosse, *History of Piracy*, p. 194.

52. George Francis Dow and John Henry Edmonds, *The Pirates of the New England Coast, 1630–1730*. New York, NY: Dover, 1996, p. 168.

53. Earle, *The Pirate Wars*, p. 206.

Chapter Four:
Asian Pirates

54. Konstam, *Piracy*, p. 288.

55. H. Warington Smyth, *Mast and Sail in Europe and Asia*. New York, NY: Dutton, 1960, p. 397.

56. Sheith Khidhir Bin Abu Bakar and Nurul Azwa Aris, "The Bugis Pirate Was a British Invention," *Free Malaysia Today*, November 6, 2017. www.freemalaysiatoday.com/category/nation/2017/11/06/the-bugis-pirate-was-a-british-invention.

57. The Editors of *Encyclopedia Britannica*, "Wako," *Encyclopedia Britannica*, accessed December 3, 2017. www.britannica.com/topic/wako.

58. Lewis, *The History of Pirates*, p. 56.

59. Lewis, *The History of Pirates*, p. 59.

60. Quoted in Hindu Janajagruti Samiti, "Sarkhel Kanhoji Angre: The Admiral of the Great Maratha Navy." www.hindujagruti.org/history/21200.html.

61. Konstam, *Piracy*, p. 295.

62. George Wingrove Cook, *China: Being "The Times" Special Correspondence from China in the Years 1857–58*. London, UK: Routledge, 1859, p. 68.

63. Nur Jale, "The Threat of Modern Day Piracy in Strategic Waters," *Eurasia Critic*, January 2009. www.eurasiacritic.com/articles/threat-modern-day-piracy-strategic-waters.

Epilogue:
Pirates at Sea and on Land
64. Jack A. Gottschalk and Brian P. Flanagan, *Jolly Roger with an Uzi: The Rise and Threat of Modern Piracy*. Annapolis, MD: Naval Institute Press, 2000, p. 24.

65. Quoted in Stefan Lovgren, "Modern Pirates Terrorize Seas with Guns and Grenades," *National Geographic*, July 6, 2006. news.nationalgeographic.com/news/2006/07/060706-modern-pirates.html.

66. Michael G. Frodl, "Hijacked Super Tanker Exposes Vulnerability of Energy Supplies," National Defense Industrial Association, March 2009. www.nationaldefensemagazine.org/archive/2009/March/Pages/HijackedSuperTankerExposes VulnerabilityofEnergySupplies.aspx.

67. Colin Freeman, "Somali Pirates Hijack First Commercial Ship in Five Years," *Telegraph*, March 14, 2017. www.telegraph.co.uk/news/2017/03/14/somali-pirates-hijack-first-commercial-ship-five-years.

68. Jamie Furlong, "Pirate Alley, Putting It in Perspective," Follow the Boat, March 9, 2010. www.followtheboat.com/2010/03/09/pirate-alley-putting-it-in-perspective.

69. Quoted in Sahal Abdulle and Rob Crilly, "Somali Fishermen Opt for Piracy's Rich Pickings," *London Times*, April 7, 2009. www.timesonline.co.uk/tol/news/world/africa/article6045092.ece.

70. Quoted in "Pirates, Inc.: Inside the Booming Somali Business," Somali Directory, August 31, 2009. www.somalidirectory.net/biz/business-news/2-pirates-incinside-the-booming-somali-business.html.

71. Quoted in Rob Walker, "Inside Story of Somali Pirate Attack," BBC, June 4, 2009. news.bbc.co.uk/2/hi/africa/8080098.stm.

72. Quoted in "UAE Steps into the Fight Against Piracy," Combined Maritime Forces, April 26, 2011. combinedmaritimeforces.com.

73. Quoted in "Definitions," Maritime Terrorism Research Center. www.maritimeterrorism.com/definitions.

74. Gottschalk and Flanagan, *Jolly Roger with an Uzi*, p. 30.

75. Quoted in "New Counter-Piracy Task Force Established," Global Security, January 8, 2009. www.globalsecurity.org/military/library/news/2009/01/mil-090108-nns02.htm.

76. Quoted in Julie Mianecki, "14 Suspected Pirates Indicted in Attack on Yacht That Left 4 Americans Dead," *Los Angeles Times*, March 11, 2011. articles.latimes.com/2011/mar/11/nation/la-na-pirates-indictment-20110311.

77. Christian Barry, "Is Downloading Really Stealing? The Ethics of Digital Piracy," *The Conversation*, April 13, 2015. theconversation.com/is-downloading-really-stealing-the-ethics-of-digital-piracy-39930.

78. Barry, "Is Downloading Really Stealing?"

79. Kal Raustiala and Chris Sprigman, "How Much Do Music and Movie Piracy Really Hurt the U.S. Economy?," *Freakonomics*, January 12, 2012. freakonomics.com/2012/01/12/how-much-do-music-and-movie-piracy-really-hurt-the-u-s-economy.

80. Michael Moyer, "Does Digital Piracy Really Hurt Movies?" *Scientific American*, May 1, 2012. www.scientificamerican.com/article/does-digital-piracy-really.

81. Nelson Granados, "How Online Piracy Hurts Emerging Artists," *Forbes*, February 1, 2016. www.forbes.com/sites/nelsongranados/2016/02/01/how-online-piracy-hurts-emerging-artists/#7647d3627774.

82. Aatif Sulleyman, "Pirate Treasure: How Criminals Make Millions from Online Streaming," *Independent*, September 19, 2017. www.independent.co.uk/life-style/gadgets-and-tech/news/piracy-streaming-illegal-feeds-how-criminals-make-money-a7954026.html.

83. Sulleyman, "Pirate Treasure."

For More Information

Books

Croce, Pat. *Blackbeard*. Philadelphia, PA: Running Press Kids, 2011.
   Readers of this book learn the history of an authentic American villain.

Hamilton, Libby, Mathieu Leyssenne, and Jason Kraft. *The Ultimate Pirate Handbook: Everything You Need to Know About Pirate Life*. Somerville, MA: Templar Books, 2014.
   The authors discuss the realities of life on a pirate ship.

Platt, Richard, and Tina Chambers. *Pirate*. London, UK: Dorling Kindersley, 2000.
   This book discusses pirates and privateers and is illustrated with photographs of weapons, ships, maps, and flags.

Witt, Stephen. *How Music Got Free: A Story of Obsession and Invention*. New York, NY: Penguin, 2016.
   Music is one of the most frequently pirated digital media. Readers learn how this crime has come to be seen as a normal part of life in the 21st century.

Yolen, Jane. *Sea Queens*. Watertown, MA: Charlesbridge, 2008.
   Yolen covers the lives and legends surrounding a variety of female pirates, including Anne Bonny, Mary Read, and Zheng Yi Sao.

Websites

International Maritime Bureau (IMB)
www.icc-ccs.org/piracy-reporting-centre
    This website gives modern piracy news and statistics,
    maps where piracy is occurring, piracy-prone areas, and more.

National Geographic: **Pirates**
www.nationalgeographic.com/search/?q=pirates
    This interactive website gives information about real historical pirates.

National Intellectual Property Rights Coordination Center
www.iprcenter.gov
    This government website explains how digital piracy harms the economy.

Pirates and Privateers: The History of Maritime Piracy
www.cindyvallar.com/pirates.html
    Run by a former librarian with research experience, this website includes
    articles about every aspect of maritime piracy, classroom activities, and links
    to other literature.

The Pirate's Realm
www.thepiratesrealm.com
    In addition to a wide range of information about pirates, this website includes
    a list of pirate museums in the United States and other countries.

Index

Picture Credits

Cover MOHAMED DAHIR/AFP/Getty Images; pp. 6–7 (background) Oleg Voronische/Shutterstock.com; p. 6 (left) Michael Fellner/Moment Open/Getty Images; p. 6 (right) Archive Photos/Getty Images; p. 7 (left) MC1 Eric L. Beauregard/Corbis via Getty Images; p. 7 (right) Rob Bouwman/Shutterstock.com; p. 9 wavebreakmedia/Shutterstock.com; p. 10 bodom/Shutterstock.com; p. 11 Popperfoto/Getty Images; pp. 15, 47 Culture Club/Getty Images; pp. 16, 29, 62 Peter Hermes Furian/Shutterstock.com; p. 17 Craig Pershouse/Lonely Planet Images/Getty Images; p. 18 DEA PICTURE LIBRARY/De Agostini Picture Library/Getty Images; p. 20 Paul Popper/Popperfoto/Getty Images; p. 22 RGR Collection/Alamy Stock Photo; p. 23 Zack Frank/Shutterstock.com; p. 26 Stephen Sweet/Alamy Stock Photo; p. 27 Oleksiy Maksymenko/All Canada Photos/Getty Images; pp. 28, 41 Stock Montage/Getty Images; p. 32 Tami Freed/Shutterstock.com; p. 33 Miriam Doerr Martin Frommherz/Shutterstock.com; pp. 35, 51 The Print Collector/Getty Images; pp. 37, 79 ROBERTO SCHMIDT/AFP/Getty Images; p. 38 Eva Bidiuk/Shutterstock.com; p. 44 BlueOrange Studio/Shutterstock.com; p. 46 Leemage/Corbis via Getty Images; p. 50 Hoiseung Jung/Shutterstock.com; p. 53 Bettmann/Bettmann/Getty Images; p. 55 whitemay/E+/Getty Images; p. 56 Fototeca Gilardi/Getty Images; p. 57 Kishivan/Shutterstock.com; p. 61 Baiterek Media/Shutterstock.com; p. 64 InkKing/Shutterstock.com; p. 66 Marzolino/Shutterstock.com; p. 68 Science History Images/Alamy Stock Photo; pp. 72, 75 Rainer Lesniewski/Shutterstock.com; p. 74 Bambu Productions/DigitalVision/Getty Images; p. 76 Moviestore collection Ltd/Alamy Stock Photo; p. 77 PJF Military Collection/Alamy Stock Photo; p. 80 MOHAMED ABDIWAHAB/AFP/Getty Images; p. 84 STRINGER/AFP/Getty Images; p. 86 David McNew/Getty Images; p. 87 360b/Shutterstock.com; p. 90 Yui Mok/PA Images via Getty Images; p. 92 pixinoo/Shutterstock.com.

About the Author

Jennifer Lombardo earned her BA in English from the University at Buffalo and still resides in Buffalo, New York, with her cat, Chip. She has helped write a number of books for young adults on topics ranging from world history to body image. In her spare time, she enjoys cross-stitching, hiking, and volunteering with Habitat for Humanity.